KEEPING *love alive*

KEEPING love alive

ANSWERS TO 100 MARRIAGE QUESTIONS

BY
KENNETH W. MATHESON

CFI
Springville, Utah

ISBN 13: 978-1-59955-245-3

Published by CFI, an imprint of Cedar Fort, Inc., 2373 W. 700 S., Springville, UT 84663
Distributed by Cedar Fort, Inc., www.cedarfort.com

Library of Congress Cataloging-in-Publication Data

Matheson, Kenneth W. (Kenneth William), 1943–
  Keeping love alive / Kenneth W. Matheson.
      p. cm.
  ISBN 978-1-59955-245-3
  1. Marriage. I. Title. II. Title: Answers to one hundred marriage
questions.

  HQ734.M4299 2009
  646.7'803--dc22

  2008048880

Cover design by Angela D. Olsen
Cover design © 2009 by Lyle Mortimer
Edited and typeset by Natalie A. Hepworth

Printed in the United States of America

10 9 8 7 6 5 4 3 2 1

Printed on acid-free paper

To my wife, Marlene,
whose encouragement, love, and support over the years have
made this book a reality.

Contents

Contents

Acknowledgments

This book is the result of the influence and assistance of many individuals. I am grateful for the extra push that the Writewise organization provided to help me see that I had a book within me; their guidance has been invaluable. I am also grateful to the many family members and friends who read the manuscript in its beginning phases and provided helpful suggestions. The sabbatical leave which I was granted by Brigham Young University provided the much-needed uninterrupted time for me to organize my thoughts and ideas. I wish to acknowledge my graduate research assistants who have assisted me in many ways. A final thanks to those at Cedar Fort Publishing for having confidence in me and the final product.

To my wife, Marlene, and our children, Marty, Marcia, Marc, Marianne, McKay, and Merrill, I express my love and appreciation for you, for teaching me over the years. Much love and appreciation is also expressed to their spouses and children.

Foreword

Even though they may not be happy in their relationships, most individuals are content to say to themselves, "My marriage is stuck where it is, and there's nothing I can do about it."

By reading this book, you will gain the necessary information to empower yourself toward a better marriage. Even if your spouse doesn't wish to work with you at this time, you can still make a significant change. By just reading the foreword of this book, you have shown interest in improving the relationship you have with your spouse.

Many couples that are beginning their life together assume that their marriage will fulfill all of their individual expectations, with little or no preparation to achieve that goal. They soon learn how naïve that notion is. Most expect their marriage to work out simply because they are in love. Soon, the pressures of life arise and then the once small, insignificant issues become points of irritation.

From reading this book, you will learn that not all differences will be resolved. Differences are a normal part of life. The goal is not to think alike, but to think together. You will also learn that some of the same problems that cause couples to divorce are also experienced by couples who are happy and content in their marriages. Why is this?

By reading *Keeping Love Alive: Answers to 100 Marriage Questions*, you will discover what it is that creates satisfaction in a marriage.

I promise that if you will read and incorporate the principles presented in this book, your marriage will improve within seven days.

Introduction

IMPORTANCE OF MARRIAGE AND FAMILIES

On their wedding day, every couple plans on having a blissful, happy, and lasting marriage. After all, they believe they are a unique couple, and the exception to any current trend or statistic. In fact, I have never met a couple who, on their wedding day, planned on getting a divorce. Yet, it's widely accepted that approximately 50 percent of first marriages end in divorce. What goes wrong? Why aren't these couples staying married?

On 24 February 2004, President George W. Bush announced the importance of marriage to the world by referring to it as "the most fundamental institution of civilization." He said, "The union of a man and woman is the most enduring human institution, honored and encouraged in all cultures and by every religious faith. Ages of experience have taught humanity that the commitment of a husband and wife to love and to serve one another promotes the welfare of children and the sanctity of society. Marriage cannot be severed from its cultural, religious, and natural roots without weakening the good influence of society. Government, by recognizing and protecting marriage, serves the interests of all."[1]

According to Olson and Olson, "Although the popularity of marriage seems to be decreasing, marriage has many positive societal, familial, and personal benefits. Married people tend to be healthier, live longer, have more wealth and economic assets, and have more satisfying sexual relationships than single or cohabiting individuals. In addition, children generally do better emotionally and academically when they are raised in two-parent families."[2]

Regardless of what many experts are saying, some people still conclude that satisfying and fulfilling marriages do not exist. It appears that society has been so preoccupied with failed marriages that little attention is being given to what makes a good marriage. Statistics show that many individuals are older when they marry, and that many decide to never marry. This could be due to the fact that problem marriages are all around us, and the negative aspects of those marriages are overwhelming to potential couples.

If we are honest with ourselves, every time we go to a wedding reception we secretly ask ourselves the question, "Will this couple make it, or will they get a divorce?"

When I have asked individuals what means the most to them, the most common answer I hear is, "My marriage and my family." We all know that marriage is challenging, difficult, and has to be worked at consistently. Everyone desires a close relationship where there is appreciation, understanding, consideration, support, and companionship. Marriage is supposed to provide such an opportunity.

Further statistical data indicates that the number of marriages has decreased over the years. In 1970, 68 percent of the population was married. In 1998, 56 percent of the population was married.[3] Trends also say that fewer people are getting married, and that people who were once married and then divorced are not re-marrying.

The number of individuals who have never been married has increased from 21 million (16 percent) in 1970 to 45 million (23 percent) in 1996. This is probably directly related to the increased number of cohabiting couples. In 1970, 500 thousand couples were living together; that number increased to 3.7 million in 1996; and over 4 million in 1998. For the United States in 2001:

- Number of marriages: 2,327,000
- Marriage rate: 8.4 per 1,000 total population
- Divorce rate: 4.0 per 1,000 population (46 reporting States and Washington D.C.)[4]

Have you ever wondered why two very good people can marry and then experience a difficult time with their marriage relationship? Even though the answer can be complex, the fundamental adjustment comes when a single person marries and has to change his thinking from "I," "me," or "mine," to "you," "us," and "ours." Ofttimes, a person does not successfully make this change of focusing on someone else's needs, but nevertheless, it is essential in making a marriage relationship work.

A newlywed couple usually says they are in love, but love alone (whatever that means) does not appear to be adequate to guarantee a successful and happy marriage. The development of relationship skills and a strong commitment from both partners are mandatory for success in any marriage.

THE IMPORTANCE OF MARRIAGE

Over the centuries, marriage and the family have remained the fundamental units of society. Marriage has been altered in its definition, and by some societies it has been done away with entirely. However, the need for legalized marriages still prevails.

For the past thirty years, marriage has been on the decline, and there appears to be little evidence to suggest any immediate change in direction.

Most authorities conclude that individuals who are happily married have healthier and longer lives than those who are not married. I refer to a statement made by John Gottman when he said, "People who are happily married live longer, healthier lives than either divorced people or those who are unhappily married."[5]

WHY THIS BOOK?

There are many books written on marriage; what's different about this one? There are three main answers to this question: (1) Over years of lecturing, people have come up to me afterwards asking for the source of certain materials I have used, or they ask the question, "Have you written a book?" Now I can refer them to this one. (2) All books written on the topic of marriage attempt to be helpful and to some degree are. The majority are usually based solely on the author's research, insights, and experiences gained from counseling couples. Other authors give advice, based solely on being married, with no professional experience to support their comments. As they give advice, they are basically saying, "This has worked for me, I know it will work for you." In contrast, this book draws upon my forty years of working with individuals and couples, my years of teaching marriage and family concepts, and it also cites other professionals and persons of authority to assist couples in formulating and implementing sound principles that can help their marriage. (3) In some other books, couples must "wade through" the entire book to find an answer to a specific question. This book is written in specific categories, including questions for quick reference that will make it easier for couples to find answers, and ideally apply the answers and concepts provided. I am fully aware that over-generalizations and inferences cannot be made about a specific couple—couples are not one-size-fits-all. Therefore, when reading both the questions and the answers, each individual needs to adapt the response to his or her own specific situation.

GETTING STARTED

I've had people ask me to refer them to a book they could read to help them with the challenges they were having. I've had others approach me stating they already have a lot of books which haven't helped, or they just haven't been able to get around to reading all of them. They want to know what I would advise them to do. These individuals make me think of the saying I once heard:

> I spent a fortune on a trampoline,
> A stationary bike and a rowing machine;
>
> Complete with gadgets to read my pulse and
> Gadgets to prove my progress results
>
> And others to show the miles I've charted,
> But they left off the gadget to get me started.

There are no quick fixes to improve a marriage. It just takes a lot of constant effort. You just have to make up your mind that you're going to put forth that effort, even when you don't feel like it. It comes down to making a choice. I hope the information provided in this book will assist you in your journey to improve your marriage.

Notes

1. Associated Press, "President Bush's Address on Protecting Marriage," *Provo Daily Herald*, February 25, 2004.

2. D. H. Olsen and A. K. Olsen, *Empowering Couples: Building on Your Strengths*, 2nd edition (Minneapolis: Life Innovations, Inc., 2000), 3.

3. U. S. Bureau Census, 1998, www.census.gov.

4. *National Vital Statistics Report*, Vol. 50, No. 8, 24 May 2002.

5. John Gottman, *The Seven Principles for Making Marriage Work: A*

Practical Guide from the Country's Foremost Relationship Expert (New York: Three Rivers Press, 1999), 4.

Abuse

Domestic violence is a broad category and can be done by a member of a family to any other member of the family. Abuse can occur between husband and wife (spouse abuse); siblings (brother/sister; brother/brother; sister/sister); or through incest (parent/child).

The National Domestic Violence Hotline defines abuse as:

- Calling bad names or putting someone down
- Shouting and cursing
- Hitting, slapping and/or pushing
- Making threats of any kind
- Jealousy and suspicion
- Keeping someone away from family and friends (isolation)
- Throwing things around the house[1]

Q: What warning signs should I be looking for if I am afraid my boyfriend, or husband, might become physically abusive?

As an abused spouse looks back from her current vantage point, she can see signs that appeared in her courting days which were not heeded. Specific warning signs in the potential spouse might include some of the following:

- Always having to be right
- Little patience with others who do not agree with him
- Angry outbursts
- Grabbing, pushing, or hitting
- Constantly apologizing and promising to do better when

inappropriate behaviors occur (This cycle repeats itself.)
- A history of violence
- Being a survivor of abuse

It is so important for a future wife not to say to herself, "He'll change; it will be different after we're married." Never marry someone to take on as a "project," expecting to rescue him from or solve his problems. Look at him for what he is and make an appropriate decision concerning your future. In most cases, what you see is what you're going to get.

Ask yourself if your partner:

- Embarrasses you with put-downs
- Controls what you do, who you see or talk to, or where you go
- Takes your money, makes you ask for money, or refuses to give you money
- Makes all of the decisions
- Tells you that you're a bad parent
- Prevents you from working or attending school
- Acts like the abuse is no big deal, it's your fault, or even denies doing it
- Intimidates you with guns, knives or other weapons
- Shoves you, slaps you, chokes you, or hits you

PHYSICAL ABUSE

Q: I was physically abused when I was a young girl. I've had some help with the abuse I suffered in the past, but I still have fear. I'm afraid I'll be unable to have a normal relationship with a husband. I've heard that many people who have been abused get into abusive relationships when they are older. What advice do you have for a person who has suffered horrible physical abuse who now wants to marry?

In this woman's case, fear of past abuse is causing anticipatory fear of the future. Her great fear of not being able to have a normal relationship is holding her back. Yet, even without the problem of past abuse, there is no guarantee of anyone having a "normal relationship." Fear holds a lot of people back from realizing their potential. The fear of failure prevents individuals from even embarking on relationships. A person in this situation should move forward very cautiously with a good deal of input from significant others around her. It would be most beneficial to her to learn from the previous help she received. She should have the goal to gain control over her life without expecting a guarantee that all will go well.

Physical, sexual, and emotional abuse are unnecessary and unwarranted. There is no justification for their presence within a marriage or family.

Q: I have been living with my husband, John, for eleven years. John has been abusive for most of our married life. Whenever he gets upset he takes out his frustrations on me. He says that if I would do things "better," he wouldn't have to "punish" me. After our fights, John always promises he will change and says he is really sorry and will not hit me again, but things haven't changed. I have never been hospitalized for the damage he's done to me, but I almost always wear long-sleeved shirts and long pants to cover the bruises—even when it's hot outside. I love my husband and I would like to work things out with him, but I am also tired of dealing with the pain that comes from the physical abuse I endure. What can I do to stop the abuse?

This situation is very complex because there are a variety of emotions involved. There are cases where the wife is the aggressor, with similar dynamics present; but the following answer will assume that the husband is the aggressor. There is never any justification for this type of repeated behavior, nor should it be tolerated.

First, the wife should remove herself from the abuse. She already said the abuse is continual and only stops for short periods of time. There are facilities where a wife (and children) can go for protection. Women who receive shelter services endure shorter periods of violence than women who do not access such services.[2]

Spouse abuse usually follows a pattern. An abusive episode occurs and then the husband goes into the "honeymoon phase," where he will apologize and make promises that his abusive behavior will never happen again. The wife buys into those promises and, for a short time, his behavior will be more appropriate. But inevitably, the behavior will recur. This behavior on a husband's part can be overcome, but a confession to a religious leader and some professional help might be needed to achieve that goal.

The wife is not there to be her husband's punching bag. If she feels she deserves this type of behavior (and she shouldn't), then she needs help just as much as the husband does. It is time for the wife to take action. She probably needs to speak with someone who can help her see the dynamics of her behavior and assist her in increasing her self-worth. The change in the husband will probably only be initiated by firmness and consistency on the wife's part.

Someone once said that in order to be treated like a doormat, you first have to lie down. This is not to say that a wife deserves to be abused. This statement implies that the wife needs to become more proactive and not tolerate any physical abuse—regardless of the justification the husband might give. Nothing she could do would justify abuse from her husband.

SEXUAL ABUSE

Q: My friend says it isn't possible to sexually abuse a spouse because it involves two married adults. I say spouse sexual abuse does exist. Why does it? Who's right?

You win the argument. There is such a thing as spouse sexual abuse, and it can be perpetrated by either the husband or the wife; but for the purposes of this discussion, we'll say that the husband is sexually abusing the wife.

It is a fallacy to say that whatever happens between a husband and wife is okay because they are married and "anything goes." This is just not true. There needs to be sensitivity and gentleness between partners, especially in their physical relationship. There needs to be understanding and tenderness in trying to meet the expectations of the partner. There needs to be communication to discover what behaviors are jointly acceptable. There should be no coercion or pressure to conform to the partner's desires. If the husband forces himself upon his wife, the behavior is wrong. If he pressures her to "experiment" with some "extreme technique or idea" that she wants no part of, then that is spouse sexual abuse.

CHILD SEXUAL ABUSE

Most abusers were abused as children. The abuse of children is so serious that firm laws have been written to protect children. If you are aware that your spouse was abused as a child, discuss this with him to discover what impact it has on his current life, and determine from the information presented if it is still an issue. Past sexual activities will often be dismissed as having minimal current effect, but that could be more denial and rationalization than reality. Be attentive to his behaviors and don't ignore any signs of possible unresolved issues. This could be obsessions with child pornography, individual late-night television watching, wanting to be alone with children, repeated references to sexual activities while growing up, and any suggestive or inappropriate comments about children.

Verbal/Emotional Abuse

Q: My wife, Janet, grew up in an emotionally abusive environment. She's aware of the problems her background has caused for her and her siblings, but she is often very demeaning to others without seeming to even notice. Janet's past has caused numerous current problems in our marriage and I am now worried about the well-being of our children. I have struggled with depression and Janet's cutting remarks have had a detrimental effect on me. I believe our children would be doing better in school if their mother was more encouraging and helpful. I want to help Janet with her problems, but I also want to approach them in a way that won't put her immediately on the defense. How do I overcome the effects of Janet's emotional abuse? How do I help our children know they are loved and special? Finally, how can I help Janet to stop being emotionally abusive?

The key here is that "Janet is aware of the problems her background has caused." Some feel the garbage they're carrying around from the past entitles them to be abusive to other people. In fact, what they're doing is projecting their anger and frustration from the past onto a current person or situation.

If a person is aware of what he is doing but doesn't care, that's one matter. If a person is aware of what he is doing and wants to stop, that's another. Sometimes an individual does not know how he comes across to others, so receiving feedback from significant others in a loving, understanding, and kind way can be helpful in the change process.

Even though there's overlap between emotional and verbal abuse, there are important differences. Emotional abuse is usually the result of verbal abuse by one spouse to the other, but it can also be more than that. When a spouse, for whatever reason, withholds or disengages from giving to the marriage, that's emotional abuse, generally used to "punish" the other spouse. When someone consistently verbally attacks his partner, that's emotional abuse.

When someone deliberately does not meet the needs of his spouse, it's easy for that spouse to personalize the behavior and jump to conclusions, which can damage the relationship.

It is extremely important to be consistent and firm with comments to an abusive spouse. If a wife tells her husband that his comments are hurtful to her and she wants him to stop, yet doesn't "hold him to it," then the abuse will probably continue. Don't make a request to an abusive husband if you don't mean it and are not willing to follow through with it.

When giving feedback to someone about his behavior, it is extremely important not to attack, belittle, or be punitive in your remarks. It's healthy to merely state one's perceptions and what effect the behavior is having on you. It's very important not to say, "You make me feel angry." Their response to that comment would be one of defensiveness and attacking back: "That's your problem." Instead, say, "I feel upset [or any other emotion] when you say that about me, because I find myself wanting to distance myself from you so I won't be hurt. I know that won't help our marriage. Could we talk about this situation in more detail without attacking each other?"

If the "soft" approach doesn't work, then be very specific and firm in what you say. "I do not deserve to be talked to like that." Stand behind your statement, and don't let the behavior happen again without responding, "Please stop, I told you I will not put up with that anymore." Once he gets the firm and consistent message from you that you deserve better and you are not going to permit his abuse anymore, change will occur. You may end up separating for a while, but he will get the message.

If for some reason the abusive behavior doesn't stop, you can ask him to leave, or you might have to leave home and stay at a shelter or with a relative or friend. Take the children with you. The perpetrator will always make it appear that his behavior is only done because of his love for you, or he will blame his actions on you. His comments are very persuasive and convincing. If you are swayed by them, his behavior will escalate. Be firm and direct in your responses, but take action when needed.

Q: Sandra and I have been married for thirty-seven years. We've weathered many hard times together, and we know we can count on each other. In recent years, however, Sandra has become more critical of everything I do. She often uses sarcastic comments that make me look like an idiot around our family members and friends. She often makes jokes about things I struggle with—things that shouldn't be discussed around others. It has gotten to the point where I often avoid Sandra because I don't want to hear the cruel things she'll say to me or about me. What can I do to help Sandra see that her words are hurtful and that they are causing problems in our marriage?

We've all said and done things to loved ones that caused pain, anguish, and other negative consequences. These are mistakes usually of judgment, not intent. However, there are times when people suppress negative feelings to the point that they come out in attacks that cause another person pain. Sandra's husband should discuss with her the feelings he is experiencing because of her comments. If she's more critical of everything "I do in recent years," she may be frustrated with numerous issues. It might be helpful to approach her and say, "Dear, I'm feeling hurt by many of the comments you've made about me recently. I'm sorry if I've offended you in some way." Prepare some concrete examples of her hurtful comments and avoid going into a discussion when your emotions are out of control, or you may begin verbally attacking her.

Since we all get frustrated at times and say things we do not mean, or we find out later that what we've said is hurtful, it is important to change our behavior when necessary.

DEFINING EMOTIONAL ABUSE

If the emotional interaction in a marriage is satisfactory to both partners and if love and enjoyment are experienced by both, there is little cause for concern since occasional pardonable mistakes do not qualify as serious emotional abuse. However, if one person believes there is a problem, there is a problem—even if the partner disagrees. Those who abuse are often content in their relationships, but they need to listen to the concerns of their partner and make corrections to resolve the issue.

Once a pattern of emotional abuse has developed, there is a risk that such hurtful behavior will escalate into physical abuse. A spouse who does not tolerate such treatment will often stop a partner from moving any further down the road toward physical abuse. There is no guarantee that things will get better by waiting, praying for the partner to change, or assuming the partner means it when he or she promises it won't happen. Both partners may need help.

I don't believe anyone would expect a person to stay in a continually abusive relationship in which she and her children are traumatized time after time. Remember, the problems of an abuser can be passed down to future generations, causing deep emotional and spiritual wounds.

HEALING FROM ABUSE

Q: I recently started a new phase in my life. I was married for twenty-two years and during that time I suffered a lot of pain, humiliation, and hurt at the hands of my ex-husband. I am still working to find the pieces of my self-respect that I worked so hard to get after being abused earlier in my life. I long to feel like a whole person again. Is it possible to heal from the effects of abuse? Is there a chance that I will ever have a healthy relationship?

A victim needs to do everything in her power to stop the abuse at the time it is occurring. Some spouses bear additional scars from being abused as innocent children. But the majority of those who suffer from abuse have both the opportunity and the responsibility to be healed so they don't offend within a relationship or suffer from future abuse all over again.

The bad choices of others do not have to completely destroy your dignity and self-concept unless you allow them to do so. It is vital for a spouse who was abused when younger to know she was not responsible for the actions of others who abused her, no matter what she was told at the time. Those who abuse only think of the moment, they don't think of what effects their behavior will have upon their victim later in life. You have the ability and power to change your attitudes and views of the abuse that occurred. There is hope for all who have been abused.

SEEK HELP

There are books, DVDs, workshops, and agencies with programs available to assist individuals involved in abuse.

Not all who have been abused need professional help. Some are able to work through the issues by themselves; others need assistance to accomplish healing. Others use the abuse to justify ineptness in their current life by saying, "I was abused, and I can't help my current functioning." In some cases, this might be just a cop-out or justification for current poor performance.

For many, a spiritual or higher power is necessary in the healing process. Developing faith and patience is a crucial step in overcoming abuse. It must always be remembered that there is hope. The past doesn't have to determine the future. You will not usually forget the abuse, but it does not have to be constantly tearing at you.

Notes

1. National Domestic Violence Hotline list, www.ndvh.org/geteducated/What-is-Domestic-Violence.

2. Subadra Panchanadeswaran, "Predicting the Timing of Women's Departure From Abusive Relationships," *Journal of Interpersonal Violence*, 22, 2007, 50–65.

Acceptance

Q: I've been married for three years. My wife knew what I liked and didn't like before we were married. For our entire married life, I have felt that she has not accepted me because of some of my issues. She is always trying to change me. I tell her that she knew my situation even before we were married, so why doesn't she just accept me for who I am? I've heard that "unconditional acceptance" is one of the main elements of a successful marriage. I feel that her love for me is conditional. What can I do?

The best example that can be given to illustrate the principle of acceptance is how a parent feels toward a child. A good parent always loves his child, but sometimes because of the behavior of the child, it takes more effort to love him. As is often stated, you always love the person but you don't always love what he or she does.

So it is in marriage. We love our spouses in spite of their undesirable behaviors. We accept our spouses for who they are, the efforts they're making to improve, and we realize the potential they have. Spouses need to accept each other unconditionally. After all, no one is perfect.

When a couple marries, each person has a set of expectations he or she hopes will be met by his or her new spouse. After the honeymoon, reality sets in and differences are noticed that weren't seen before. It's natural to apply pressure to your spouse to change, so your expectations will be met. It's okay to let your partner know what your expectations are, but it's not okay to become dogmatic in having them met. I have even heard a husband say to his wife, "If you love me, you will change."

Never put this kind of pressure on your spouse. This kind of language has nothing to do with love; rather, it has everything to do with greed and selfishness. Accept your spouse the way he is and tell him how much you appreciate his qualities. Constantly focus on what you do have, rather than on what you don't have. If you don't do this, you will always feel cheated.

We can't force others to change, nor can we hope they will change if we make them feel guilty enough. Trying to change someone usually ends in a struggle, resentment, or rage. Couples need to learn how to deal with incompatibilities. Ultimately, the desire to change has to come from within the individual.

The opposite of acceptance is criticism and judgment. When we find fault in others' behaviors, we are usually projecting an intolerance of the same behaviors found in ourselves. We need to accept others for who they are, including their weaknesses. It's a total package. It's okay to tell your spouse that while you love him, he sometimes pushes your buttons, and you just want to make him aware of it. By doing this, your spouse is aware of the impact his trait has on you, and he can work to modify the behavior in order to not be so annoying to you. Definitely share feelings and perceptions so resentful feelings don't begin to fester, but do it in a loving, kind way, rather than becoming rigid and attacking your spouse over the matter.

When we feel our partner accepts us, our self-esteem rises. A recent study examined how perception of a partner's acceptance and love affects professional success. Both members of 154 couples completed a diary for twenty-one days. The findings revealed that men and women with low self-esteem felt more accepted and loved by their partner on days when their professional lives were marked by success, and women with low self-esteem felt less accepted and loved on days when their professional lives were marked by failure. No such spillover effects emerged for people high in chronic self-esteem.[1]

In summary, when the husband is successful at work, he perceives that his wife accepts him more than if he was not successful at work. It almost sounds like a self-fulfilling prophecy. Ideally we should not let success at work be such a determining factor of our spouse's acceptance of us. Unconditional acceptance of your spouse is necessary in order to deal with incompatibilities, irreconcilable differences, and unsolvable problems.

Notes

1. S. L. Murray, D. W. Griffin, and P. Rose, "For Better or Worse? Self-Esteem and the Contingencies of Acceptance in Marriage." *Personality and Social Psychology Bulletin*, 32, 2006, 866–80.

Addictions

There are many kinds of addiction, such as alcohol, drugs, smoking, stealing, gambling, sex, and pornography to name a few. It is not the purpose of this book to present an exhaustive critique of each type of addiction, but rather to present the problems addiction can present to an individual and a marriage. The addiction of pornography will be discussed to help illustrate some principles, dynamics, and concepts that can also be applied to the other addictions.

PORNOGRAPHY

Q: I have been married for seven years to a wonderful man, and we have three children. He is successful in his work and has had positions of responsibility within our church. We had the "normal" adjustments to make in our marriage, but I thought everything was going okay. Then one night my husband mentioned that he wanted to talk with me about an important matter. He then told me that he had a severe pornography addiction. I was totally devastated and crushed. Why was I so naïve and how could I have prevented this?

While there is no foolproof way of anticipating this problem in your marriage, the following are some ways to detect if someone has a pornography addiction.

- Date for a long enough period to get to know one another. This is crucial because you are able see each other in a variety of situations.

- Open communication and trust after marriage is important so you can discuss pornography and other issues together, openly and honestly.
- If your partner pressures you to be involved in strange or bizarre acts, you should be concerned about why he is pressuring you.
- If your husband spends long periods of time on the computer late into the night, this behavior should be an alarm for you.
- Pornography is widespread and is entirely and negatively destructive of an individual and to the marriage. Anyone who says it's not is rationalizing and in denial.

Even though many pornography addicts are very good at hiding their habits, pornography can negatively impact self-esteem, which will spill over into the marriage relationship.

The word addiction is used rather than "habit." It is difficult to just stop an addiction. There are some individuals who have an "addictive personality." Whatever their addiction, they have probably tried numerous times to stop the addiction without success. Their addiction consumes their thoughts, feelings, and time. Their life seems to revolve around their addiction. They are constantly in denial about their addiction. They believe they can stop the addiction any time they choose, but then they don't.

What can a wife do if the addiction continues?

1. She can continue believing his lies and deceitfulness, hoping that someday he will come to his senses.
2. She can give her husband an ultimatum with a specific time frame. It is important to not give an ultimatum if you are not willing to follow through with it.
3. She can get some outside help from either a professional or church leader. There are many organizations conducting educational programs and groups. Preferably, attend these with your spouse together so both of you can know what role you will play in the recovery process. If your husband is unwilling to attend, you can go alone.

Don't become apathetic and do nothing when confronted with the issue of pornography. Be assertive and discover resources for help. Know also that recovery takes time and patience.

OVERCOMING AN ADDICTION

Regardless of the addiction, an individual needs to gain control over his life. Using pornography as the example, and the husband as the addicted person, the following are suggestions to overcome this destructive habit:

1. Realize the strong force, attraction, or drive behind the habit. It has probably been a part of the husband's life for years. Also understand that many attempts to overcome it have failed.

2. Be aware that one's self-esteem is not enhanced because of the behavior; rather, it is deflated and bruised, no matter what rationalizations are presented. The individual feels like a prisoner to the addiction.

3. Regardless of the origin, length, or excuse, the individual can be empowered and the addictive behavior overcome. Patience and hope need to be constantly present.

4. Prior to a pornographic experience, self-deception and rationalization are strong. Pornography doesn't just happen. The person needs to sit down at the computer, type the login information, wait a few moments, then type in additional information before he arrives at the desired site. All this time, he is saying to himself, "I'm just going to see what has changed." "I'm not doing harm to anyone." "This is not as bad as people say it is." "What problem will one more time cause—after all, I just viewed pornography a few days ago, no big deal." He is self-justifying his actions. He is focusing on the momentary "buzz" that he will experience. Inevitably, when the "buzz" or "thrill" is over, reality will set in and a "crash" will occur. He will dislike himself, feel awful, and experience an emotional "low."

5. The cycle of self-deception occurring before the "buzz" needs to be broken. He needs to say to himself: "Would I be doing this behavior if my church leader or parents were standing at my side?" "If I continue my behavior, how will I feel about myself an hour from now?" In other words, instead of focusing on the build up to the momentary "buzz," the focus is shifted to the time frame after the peak of the excitement.

6. Open and honest communication with one's spouse will greatly increase the trust level.

7. There also needs to be a spiritual component involved in the recovery process.

8. Obtain counseling and literature to assist in the recovery process.

Overcoming any addiction requires individual determination, perseverance, and the support and patience of many individuals. For some, overcoming an addiction occurs quickly; for others, a longer time with some relapses along the way is necessary. Attending groups and following the counsel of professionals and spiritual advisors can be especially helpful. Regardless of the support an individual may receive, the decision to change is ultimately his.

Adoption

Q: We've been married for three years and have not been able to get pregnant. We have gone through the emotional cycles of feeling guilty, angry, and persecuted; then blaming God for our predicament; and then finally becoming humble and accepting our circumstance. We are now considering adoption. What are the pros and cons of adopting infants, versus adopting older children? What about adopting children from other countries?

Not being able to become pregnant can be a severe trial for couples. They have the expectation that when they are ready to begin their family, everything will go smoothly. Some couples become pregnant without much effort. Others aren't so "automatic." They have to subject themselves to intrusive and expensive tests to discover the cause of their inability to conceive.

Even though this situation is sorrowful, there is a blessing that comes from it. Many children are born to single mothers who cannot care for them, and infertile couples can take those children into their homes and hearts.

As you begin to consider adoption, you'll have many questions. Are you willing to commit to a child for a lifetime? Remember, your motivations have to be based on what is in the best interest of the child, not your own. You have to be financially and emotionally ready to care for a child.

Many different types of children are waiting to be adopted. As you make your decision, consider your age, the number of children already living in your home, and your financial means. Are you most interested in adopting a newborn or an older child? Do you have the desire to adopt a child from another country, and are you willing to go through the additional paperwork of adopting internationally?

When you adopt an infant, you will be present as the child develops and you are there to bond with him or her. Another advantage of adopting a newborn is that you may obtain a health history from the baby's birth parents.

The cons of adopting an infant are that you have to be ready to take placement at any time. The birth parents could possibly change their minds, and you could possibly have some openness with the birth mother after placement which you didn't desire. This decision is made before the adoption takes place. If the adoptive parents don't want to have an open adoption, they aren't forced into it. They might lose that particular child, if the birth mother was set on an open adoption, but they won't be made to have a relationship they don't want.

When you adopt an older child, you can predict when placement will occur, the child may already have routines established such as sleeping through the night, plus you may know if the child has any behavioral issues.

One con of adopting an older child is not knowing his complete background. The child may have experienced a traumatic event in his life and may have problems bonding with caregivers. Agencies are usually very good about providing all the information they can about the children. You'll get a file with various reports from everyone who has been involved with that child, and he will have a medical workup done by the agency or state. Your child is thoroughly evaluated, and you are given classes to know how to handle different types of situations.

The pros of adopting internationally include having a closed adoption, adopting a child who is older, being able to plan when placement occurs, and having another culture included in your family.

The cons of adopting internationally include more paperwork, no history on the child, having to teach the child a new language, and issues related to the child's living in a depressing environment.

Anger

Q: Whenever my spouse and I talk our tempers flare and we are unable to agree on anything. I've tried being rational, but every time I bring up a behavior or attitude she needs to change, my spouse becomes very defensive, angry, and rude. I'm sorry to admit that I act the same way whenever she has similar concerns. How can we diffuse some of our anger and stop heading toward divorce?

SOURCES OF ANGER

When a couple cannot seem to agree on anything and emotions are running high, the real issue generally lies in past resentment that has been building. When a spouse suppresses and holds onto frustrations, his or her emotional temperature can be compared to water on the stove. The growing frustration, like heating water, can only be contained to a point. If it isn't taken off the stove in time, the argument explodes, even if the topic is not that emotionally charged. Developing self-awareness and learning how to lower each individual's "emotional temperature" will go a long way in helping couples to be more rational, rather than defensive and angry.

Everyone reacts differently. Our reactions are usually determined by past experiences, by the value we place upon the subject being discussed, by pressures currently being felt, or by feelings toward other individuals involved. Timing, basic communication, and problem-solving skills would be helpful to address this couple's issues. I would ask each member of the couple: "What's going on inside of you right now?" and "What meaning do you attach to what your partner just stated, or how they just behaved?" These types of questions change the focus from the topic being discussed to how the couple is relating to each other. It's easy to become defensive when attacked, but having a clear head and control of one's emotions are necessary to overcome the hurdle of constant arguing.

CONTROLLING ANGER

Controlling our anger should be one of the first things we learn to do in our marriage. There are individuals who blame their anger on their heritage, their family background, their hair color, or their current situation. Ideally, human beings should be *actors* and not *reactors*. However, much of our time is spent being reactive instead of proactive. A very upset lady came into my office. When I asked her why she was angry, her response was, "Because my husband is upset with me." Just think how many times our temperament is a reaction to a perceived "trigger" that we use to justify our emotional response.

Individuals need to take charge of their emotional reactions to situations and, especially, to other people. I have learned over the years that nothing is ever accomplished by a raised voice. An individual cannot control how others behave, but he or she can control his or her response. It is important that individuals have enough self-awareness to know when they are out of control, so they can by saying, "I can't handle that right now," or "Can I get back to you?" A delay in response might allow the individual to cool down, gain composure, and then respond objectively rather than emotionally. Learning to control your temper can be accomplished with practice.

Q: Rosa says her husband, Clint, can be so thoughtless at times. Clint comes home from work and immediately begins to say or do things that are hurtful. She reminds him that just because he had a "bad day at work," he doesn't have the right to yell and be impatient with her. "He's critical of me the minute he walks in the house. I don't look forward to him coming home." Rosa admits that Clint does not realize the negative impact his actions are having on her—she's never told him because she doesn't want to start a big fight. She asks, "What can I do? It's getting worse and something needs to be done."

SELF-AWARENESS AND ANGER

How typical this scenario is. Everyone needs to raise his level of self-awareness and realize how he comes across to others. First of all, Clint needs to realize that when he comes home, he needs to leave his work at work and not bring it with him. Sensitivity to others may not be a high priority in his work environment. The focus might be just getting a job done, but at home, he needs to demonstrate tenderness and sensitivity. Second, Rosa has a responsibility to appropriately share her feelings so Clint's awareness of his behavior can increase. After all, he might just say, "I didn't know I was bothering you. Why didn't you ever say anything?" If Rosa would share her perceptions in a non-attacking and peaceful way, this situation could be addressed in a positive manner.

Feelings of frustration are natural; they are a part of being human. However, anger is usually a secondary emotion and is not the true problem. Anger usually is overriding another emotion. If a wife were to normally pick up her husband at 5:30, but didn't show up until 6:15, he might become annoyed and then angry. But more likely, the husband might begin by feeling irritated, disappointed, or even unimportant. After all, what could be more important than meeting your significant other after work and on time? With every passing minute, the husband's emotional temperature rises. At a certain point, his frustration might turn to concern about her well-being and safety. Was she in an accident on her way to get him?

Anger is how his frustration and irritation is conveyed to his wife. Regardless of whether the anger is a primary or secondary emotion, it can be controlled. Each of us must constantly work on the following areas:

- Controlling our temper
- Bridling negative emotions
- Developing patience
- Being a peacemaker
- Abstaining from vulgarity
- Abstaining from violent behavior

If we didn't learn to control these emotions in childhood, we must work on them as adults. Parental modeling is a major influence in teaching anger management. Children should be taught that it is okay to feel upset and that, in and of itself, being upset does not make them bad children. However, children must also learn that they cannot always act on negative emotions. How we deal with frustration and anger is what makes the difference between being in control versus being out of control.

PREVENTING ANGER

People must learn to manage their emotions before trying to engage in any dialogue. When an individual is angry, he tends to think irrationally. This can lead to inappropriate comments and, in some cases, harm to the other partner. To help keep control of our emotions, the following guidelines should be helpful.

1. **Take time to cool down.** This involves removing yourself from the "stressor," which provides an opportunity for you to gain control and a new perspective on the situation.

2. **Do something physical.** This can take the form of jogging, walking, bicycling, or any kind of aerobic activity. This activity alone will not solve the problem, but it will help alleviate pent-up emotions so they are not the driving force behind any comments we make to our spouse. The issues must still be discussed after exercise.

3. **Do something constructive.** One woman tells the story of how her father found a small box with doilies in it after his wife died. The daughters told their father that the mother used to crochet the doilies when she was upset with him. He was very relieved to see only two doilies in the box. As they continued to search her belongings, they came upon a box underneath the mattress and found quite a bit of money in it. When the father asked about it, the daughters replied that the money was that which his wife received from selling her doilies.

Q: Gary and I get along well most of the time. However, whenever work or life gets really stressful, our relationship suffers. For some reason, when Gary has a bad day at work, he'll come home speaking and acting so rudely that I'm unable to stand being near him. After Gary's rude behavior, I get on edge and am rude back to him. I know that if we can help one another with our problems, we'll get along better. Do you have any advice on how we can control our emotions in the beginning so that we won't get into that hurtful, rude cycle anymore?

A lot of husbands feel justified in being rude upon coming home from a bad day at work. This type of behavior on the husband's part is called, "kicking the cat syndrome." His wife and family have done nothing, but because he had a bad day, he now takes his emotions out on his family. What wife would want a husband who comes home and immediately begins attacking his family members? I would assume that not many husbands would want to have their family on the defensive in his presence. "The size of a man (his wisdom) may be measured by the size of the things that make him angry."[1]

One of the most well-known and effective methods of helping a couple in this situation is to utilize the "I" message. If someone is attacking you, gently tell him, "I feel upset when you speak to me that way." By using this approach, you are not attacking the other person; you are factually stating his behavior and listing the emotion you are experiencing. By stating the emotion at the beginning of the discussion, the emotion is less likely to build and become disruptive to the communication that is taking place. In return, the other party is less likely to feel attacked and become defensive.

Impatience with the imperfections of a spouse can cause a lot of problems, but maybe it's not so much a question of imperfection as it is a difference of ideas.

Everyone can learn to develop a pleasant disposition—an even temperament. As individuals, we are not locked into a specific way of behaving. One of Clint's problems was bringing his work frustrations home. The following story illustrates how a husband successfully leaves his work and troubles outside the front door.

THE TROUBLE TREE

The carpenter I hired to help me restore an old farmhouse had just finished a rough first day on the job. A flat tire made him lose an hour of work, his electric saw quit, and now his ancient pickup refused to start.

While I drove him home, he sat in stony silence. Upon arriving, he invited me in to meet his family. As we walked toward the front door he paused briefly at a small tree, touching the tips of the branches with both hands. After opening the door he underwent an amazing transformation. His tanned face was wreathed in smiles and he hugged his two small children and gave his wife a kiss. Afterward he walked me to the car. We passed the tree and my curiosity got the better of me. I asked him about what I had seen him do earlier.

"Oh, that's my trouble tree," he replied. "I know I can't help having troubles on the job, but one thing's for sure, troubles don't belong in the house with my wife and the children. So I just hang them up on the tree every night when I come home. Then in the morning I pick them up again.

"Funny thing is," he smiled, "when I come out in the morning to pick them up, there aren't nearly as many as I remember hanging up the night before."

—Author Unknown

Notes

1. J. K. Morley, http://www.tentmaker.org/Quotes/lifewisdomquotes. htm.

Beliefs

Q: My wife and I were raised under very different circumstances. We have varying views on how to raise children, how to run a household, and even on how to properly act in a marriage relationship. I know the conflict in our marriage could be greatly reduced if we could come together on our philosophies about life, raising children, and everything else. What suggestions do you have to help us support each other and increase the number of beliefs we share?

Q: I come from a strict Jewish background. My family has always been serious about religion, and I believe what I have learned about my Jewish faith. I am dating a woman who comes from a staunch Catholic background. We love each other and have talked extensively about getting married, but we argue about which church to get married in. I believe our marriage would go more smoothly if she converted to my religion. How can I help her become more interested? What do the experts say about two people marrying from two different religious backgrounds?

Most religious leaders admonish their members to marry within their own denomination. However, when a couple is in love, they feel that love will keep them together or that they will be able to convert the spouse to their own religion. In some cases, a potential spouse even promises to join another church after marriage, but never follows through with that promise. Even though toleration does exist, different beliefs can cause great stress in relationships. Think about the various religious events that might cause stress. In what church should the child be baptized? Which church should the child attend?

During the time that parents are dealing with their religious differences, the issue of what church the children should attend needs to be addressed. Since there will be no one right answer for every situation, each couple must look at their particular circumstances and decide from there. Some of the factors to keep in mind are the child's age, the child's wishes, and the child's friends. Never should a child become the "ping-pong ball" or the scapegoat of the parents' frustrations and irritations. Compromise and support, rather than forcefulness and domination, should be used when making decisions.

The simple answer is for the husband to live his own faith, thereby showing his wife how important it is to him, rather than focusing on her lack of conversion. However, this question should have been addressed prior to marriage. The marriage might run more smoothly if the couple shares the same religious beliefs. However, that in and of itself is no guarantee of happiness. A couple could belong to the same religious denomination yet have different levels of commitment and activity.

You must remember that you cannot force someone to believe the way you do. Pressure and guilt cause resentment and resistance. At the time of the marriage, the husband decided that the wife's love and their relationship were more important than their religion.

If the husband constantly brings up the issue of religion instead of endearing his wife toward his church, he will, in reality, push his wife away from membership. The couple needs to focus on the beliefs and values they have in common, rather than using the religion as a point of irritation. The husband needs to focus on the positive aspects of his marriage so the relationship can be constructive. His decision is now to do the best he can in the marriage, even with different values and belief systems and church membership.

Couples should support each other in their respective church activities, even though they aren't a member of the other's faith. They could attend church dinners, athletic events, scouting recognition nights, and athletic events together without the spouse feeling uncomfortable. Within the home, regardless of religious affiliation, a weekly night devoted to family participation can be held; family prayers can still be said; religious teachings of common values adhered to by both faiths can be shared.

Good values are not just found in one religion. Honesty, integrity, chastity, service, and the golden rule can be modeled and taught in homes where the parents are working together to raise children who will make a contribution to society.

It's important that the mother and father keep their relationship of love and respect for each other alive and vibrant. Their communication with each other needs to be open, honest, and appropriate so that when issues arise, problems can be resolved. A person should not marry another individual with the expectation that one will join the other's church.

Blended Families

Q: Since my wife died, I have been so lonely. About six months ago, I decided to start dating again. This has been a tough process for me and for my children. However, I recently met the most wonderful woman. She was divorced about four years ago, and she also has two children. We have been talking about the possibility of getting married. I am concerned about meshing our two families. What kinds of problems are common in blended families? How can some of these blended family problems be addressed?

In a published research study, it was found that the most frequently reported issue couples argue about in first marriages was money, and in remarriages it was conflict about children.[1]

When discussing blending families, children are definitely at the center of the conversation. Every situation is different based on how the first marriage ended, the time that has passed since the marriage ended, lingering feelings from the first marriage, children involved, the ex-spouse (if a factor), and many other issues. If one of the spouses died, the surviving spouse should have ample time to work through his grief and mourning. The time frame varies in every case.

Unity

Husbands and wives need a strong relationship. No matter the makeup of their children, parents need to spend time together and continually discuss important issues.

Families need to share goals and spend time together. It is vital that they attend church together, practice their religion in their home, hold family prayer and family council, work on projects together, engage in leisurely activities, and start new traditions.

Stepparents need to be patient and concentrate on building a new relationship with each child. Children should not have to compete for a parent's love; both parents need to show love and exercise patience. Each child has his own issues regarding having his "real father" replaced with a "new dad." This cannot be forced. Respect is earned and takes time.

COMMUNICATION

It is important that the newly married couple have open communication and regularly define responsibilities, establish boundaries, resolve emotional issues, and talk openly about wounds caused by death or divorce. They should always encourage their children to express their thoughts and feelings on the topic.

Each spouse should respect memories and feelings family members may have about a loved one who has passed on. Be sensitive and respect family members who are still recovering from the pain and suffering caused by divorce or death.

INTIMACY

In order for intimacy in a new marriage to be fulfilling, both husband and wife must practice understanding, care, concern, and consideration. Be open in a kind and sensitive way. Intimacy is necessary—even if they don't plan on having more children, or if the couple has reached a certain age. Always put the role of intimacy in perspective. Some believe that a positive, intimate relationship makes for a good marriage. Others believe that a good marriage makes for a positive, intimate relationship. You really need both perspectives. Romance is important to the marriage. However, concern, gentleness, and patience for one's spouse will do more for the marriage relationship than constantly focusing on or forcing the physical aspect of the relationship.

FINANCES

All family members need to understand the family's financial situation and monetary constraints. This does not mean that the parents need to discuss specific details of the income, but it does mean that a sound budget needs to be established and financial priorities need to be set. Review the family's financial situation often and discuss the role each family member plays in achieving a balanced budget.

CHILDREN

As previously mentioned, the most common issues couples deal with in second marriages involve children. If there are children in the newly blended family who don't like you, remember that in their eyes, either you or your spouse is the outsider. You are the new dimension in the family system. In most cases, the children love their mother and father and still want them to be together. They resent a new parent intruding in their family. For the most part, they don't understand why a divorce or death occurred, or why their custodial parent had to remarry to be happy. After all, the original family was doing just fine. The key is to help the new parent make the stepchildren feel important. You must help them realize you are not trying to take their original parent's place; rather, you are there because you love their mother or father. Express your positive feelings toward them, but do not push yourself on them. Do not force them to love you because you are now their father or mother. Always look at everything from the children's perspective. Help them feel important. Include them in family decisions and seek their opinions when appropriate. It will take time to become used to a new household.

Discipline is effective only after a bond of love, affection, trust, and care has been firmly established. In the absence of love by a new parent, discipline can be interpreted by children as rejection.

Newly married parents should reach a consensus early in marriage regarding proper behavior and methods of discipline. Be united as parents in these matters. Developing the skills of patience, listening, and showing respect for differences in matters of discipline will help the couple to be reconciled and develop one unified standard. It is necessary to be sensitive to the children who divide their time between two homes and two sets of rules. Give them time to adjust and internalize what is expected.

Having family activities, holding parent-child interviews, and attending church together will give parents opportunities for teaching, correcting, and reinforcing accepted behavior. Sometimes it's helpful, especially at the beginning of a blended family, for the biological parent to be the voice of authority for both parents—at least until the stepparent gains the confidence and love of the children.

With firm resolve, consistently and fairly enforce rules and consequences. Don't allow children to divide or manipulate you as parents. Don't treat the children as "his" and "hers;" rather, treat them as "our children." Children will often say, "You are not my father." When this occurs, you have the opportunity to teach them correct principles. Help the children realize that you recognize you are not their biological father, but you are now fulfilling the role of father by taking care of them, feeding them, and so forth. All are struggling with this new arrangement, so be patient. Don't force the issue by saying, "Well, I am now your dad, and you are living in my house and will do what I say." This will only push the child further away. Remember, you are not trying to force the children into a specific way of thinking or behaving; you are trying to help them take charge of their own life (as age appropriate).

Former Spouses

Try to maintain a good relationship with the former spouse for the sake of the children, and for the spouse's sake. Remember, you will always have a relationship with the former spouse if children are involved. If problems arise with the former spouse, handle them privately.

It is imperative to encourage and support ongoing relationships between children and the biological parent who no longer lives with them. Do not verbally criticize a former spouse in front of the children. This will put a wedge between you and the former spouse, and you just might be the loser.

Realize that the children will deal with challenges while adjusting to the newly created family. Help your current family unite to help fill the void of the missing persons in your child's life. Reassure the child that he is not to blame for the divorce or death.

Remember that children of a blended family can find themselves with twice as many grandparents, aunts and uncles, and cousins as they had in their former family. Each parent, meanwhile, has acquired another set of in-laws. All these individuals make up the children's extended family and, to a degree, are interested in a relationship with the children. Visits, family gatherings, and observance of holidays require compromise and planning.

Keep in mind that family success requires perseverance and stamina, both physically and spiritually. Sacrifices must be made, and spiritual resources must be called upon.[2]

I have discovered from my experience in working with blended families that the more difficulties spouses experience in their roles of spouse, parent, and stepparent, the less they are satisfied with their marriage relationship. Even though this seems obvious, it does confirm that the other roles assigned to the stepparent cannot be ignored. How those roles are carried out will strongly influence the marriage relationship. I sometimes hear the comment, "I love you, but the pressures of the children are causing me to have second thoughts about us."

Sometimes couples who remarry are weighed down with concerns that stem from unresolved issues in their previous marriage. By acknowledging the influence of their previous marriage, couples are able to work through these issues and focus more attention on their current relationship.

Notes

1. Scott M. Stanley, Howard J. Markman, and Sarah W. Whitton, "Communication, Conflict, and Commitment: Insights On the Foundations of Relationship Success from a National Survey," *Family Process*, 41 (4), 2002, 659–75.

2. Adapted from Robert E. Wells, "Uniting Blended Families," *Ensign*, Aug. 1997, 24.

Career and Family

Q: I have been working outside our home for several years now. My children range from elementary school age to high school, and until recently, they have all been doing fairly well. Stress levels have really risen with work, and I have also gotten several calls from some of my children's teachers regarding behavior problems. The duties and pressures I feel from work and home are really overwhelming. My husband says he is willing to help, but I have to tell him every step in order to get things done around the house. He doesn't anticipate what needs to be done, and when he does, he doesn't do it as thoroughly as I would like. I know maternal employment can be such a touchy subject. What advice can you give me on being a working mother, and on helping my husband to understand how to best help at home? According to the experts, what impact does maternal employment have on a family and marriage?

When a couple begins a life together, they also begin a lifetime of careers. There is the career of being a student, and while being a student, also being either a full- or part-time provider. If both husband and wife are finishing school, shared responsibilities are necessary. Upon graduation, possible further education might be needed. At some point along the continuum, children enter into the picture. At this stage, the couple needs to discuss working and family responsibilities. Financial pressures are constantly present. Decisions need to be made relative to the husband engaging in a part-time job in addition to his regular job, if needed. Does the wife seek employment either in the home or out of the home? How long will this employment last? What are the consequences of such decisions? How old are the children, how many hours will be spent away from home, and who will care for them? The couple needs to look at all these issues objectively.

A couple needs to sit down and discuss expectations surrounding the various stages in their career development. Usually, husbands and wives copy expectations related to the employment patterns modeled by their own parents. If the wife's mother worked outside the home, she might expect to do so as well. A couple needs to sit down and discuss why it is important that their individual views should be carried out the way they desire.

WORKING MOTHERS

Working outside the home, raising children, and maintaining a marriage creates a lot of stress, which, in turn, will most likely create resentment between the husband and the wife. There is one major question that needs to be asked: "Is it financially and emotionally profitable, after looking at all aspects of the wife's employment, for her to work?" Being objective when looking at this question will help resolve many of the issues.

Throughout the feminist movement, although some very important rights were given, the role of women was devalued in many ways. An article in *Newsweek* in 2003 entitled "She Works, He Doesn't," concludes that "the number of American families in which the sole wage earner is the woman is small, but many economists think it's growing. . . . 54 percent of Americans know a couple where the woman is clearly the major wage earner and the man's career is secondary. . . . Women have always worked, of course. But as economic conditions and social expectations have evolved over the millenniums, so have gender roles in marriage." Further statistics show that 25 percent of the respondents said that it is generally "not acceptable for a wife to be the major wage earner. . . . 34 percent of men say that if their wife earned more money, they'd consider quitting their job or reducing their hours. . . . 50 percent of women say that when it came time to choose a mate, they considered his earning potential 'not at all important.' "[1]

Is it any wonder why opinions concerning earning power vary so much? The pendulum is definitely swinging from its position fifty years ago.

In the October 2001 issue of *Journal of Marriage and Family Therapy*, the authors interviewed many dual-income couples and asked how they adapted, adjusted, and survived. Here is the list of ten strategies for finding a balance of work and family.

1. Value family.
2. Strive for partnership.
3. Derive meaning from work.
4. Maintain work boundaries.
5. Focus and produce while at work.
6. Take pride in dual earning.
7. Prioritize family fun.
8. Live simply.
9. Make decisions proactively.
10. Value time.[2]

Results from various research studies almost suggest that working women experience significantly higher marital adjustments, more marital hassles, and more unhappiness. Nonworking women generally experienced more marital satisfaction and fulfillment.

What effect does a working mother have on a home? The answer to this question can be completely different from one family to the next. There are so many variables and dynamics that can be discussed, such as the reason she is working, the type of work she is doing, the hours of her employment, the support of family members, and the ages of the children and the role of the father. For example, if the mother is working and does not have her husband's support, it might affect his self-esteem and the kids may think their father is less competent.

Husbands and wives can work together to make a dual-income family work, if they are both willing to do their part around the house and with the children. Part of that helping has to be placed on the husbands shoulders. Many husbands believe their job is to earn the money and the wife's job is to take care of the home and children. The husband comes home and disconnects from the wife by watching TV or sitting in front of the computer. Husbands need to become more domestic and help around the house. Chores around the house are *our* chores, not *your* chores. With this change of thinking, he will assist with *our* chores, and not help you with *your* chores. This is especially needed when both partners are working outside the home. New rules are needed to make the home run smoothly. Rules are not based on what happened in the family of origin. Do whatever is necessary to establish equality within the home.

Notes

1. "She Works, He Doesn't," *Newsweek*, May 12 2003, 45–52.

2. "Ten Adaptive Strategies for Family and Work Balance: Advice from Successful Families," *Journal of Marriage and Family Therapy*, Oct. 2001, 445–58.

3. J. Neeta and R. Gunthey, "Marital Adjustment and Problems Among Working Women" *Social-Science-International*, Vol. 17 (1), Jan. 2001, 55–58.

Challenges

Q: My wife and I are reasonably good people and are trying to do things right, but life is still so hard sometimes. After a few short years of marriage, my wife got into a serious car accident and was badly injured. Her physical and mental states have changed drastically. What can I do to improve our marriage and help her understand that I still love her even after the changes? What advice do you have for couples where one spouse has unforeseen physical or mental changes? Why do good Christian people who are trying to do what is right still struggle in their marriages?

Stories such as this are not uncommon. How tragic it is to see the life of a partner change so drastically. How commendable for the husband to be by her side to support her and help her. He must realize that his wife is also struggling with the changes that have taken place. The "normal life" she had envisioned has now changed. Her dreams have been shattered. Her goals have been altered. Even the strongest person has to make significant changes in his attitude and expectations, and has to adjust to the new life that lies ahead.

One of the first things the husband needs to realize is to not force an attitude change. Do not lecture her. Let this change be gradual, yet permanent. The best way for this to occur is for the husband to be steadfast in his resolve to be by her side and demonstrate his unconditional love for her—no matter what. She is aware she has changed from who she was when they married, and probably believes that the husband would want out of the marriage. She is trying to make it easy on him to exit. But to his credit, he is not budging. Together, new plans, goals, and expectations need to be made. The destination is still attainable, but the mode of achieving it has changed. Adjustments will need to be made between the husband and wife, albeit at different speeds and diverse ways.

TYPES OF CHALLENGES

Challenges in marriage are normal and no couple can escape experiencing them. The issue becomes, will we as a couple let the challenges tear the relationship apart or bring us together? Some of the most common challenges pulling marriages and families apart are negative family relationships, broken homes, financial pressures, eating disorders, substance abuse, pornography, lowering of values, immodest clothing, dishonoring the Sabbath day, and low self-esteem.

The goal is not to totally do away with challenges, but to learn how to minimize and deal with them effectively. Challenges and trials are part of living. Overcoming and conquering them brings self-, couple-, and family-satisfaction; growth; and empowerment.

A marriage consists of sequential stages: newlyweds, parents of young children, parents of adolescent teens, midlife crisis for each partner, empty nesters, grandparents, and senior citizens. Each stage brings its own unique challenge and has to be dealt with differently. No one can say, "This is what you are experiencing, because we have also experienced it. This is how to solve it. Our solution worked for us and it will work for you." That would be like saying to someone who needs glasses: "Here, use mine. They've worked for me; I know they will work for you." Because people are different, the dynamics and solutions to problems are different. Prescribed solutions won't work, but developing self-awareness through self-talk will. This skill will help formulate new approaches to each new challenge and help couples choose the best solution and implement it.

Sometimes the challenges appear sooner than expected. The following story is told of a young couple who got married and went on their honeymoon, and when reality set in, the newly married woman was not quite ready to handle the responsibilities of the home.

> When the newlyweds got back from their honeymoon, the bride immediately called her mother.
> "Well," said her mother, "so how was the honeymoon?"
> "Oh, Mama," she replied, "the honeymoon was wonderful! So romantic . . ." Suddenly she burst out crying. "But, Mama, as soon as

we returned, Sam started using the most horrible language—things I'd never heard before! I mean all these awful four letter words! You've got to take me home. Please, Mama!"

"Sarah, Sarah," her mother said, "Calm down! You need to stay with your husband and work this out. Now, tell me, what could be so awful? What four letter words?"

"Please don't make me tell you, Mama," wept the daughter. "I'm so embarrassed, they're just too awful! Come get me, please!"

"Darling, baby, you must tell me what has you so upset. Tell your mother these horrible four letter words!"

Still sobbing, the bride said, "Oh, Mama . . . he used words like dust, wash, iron, work, cook . . ."

"I'll pick you up in twenty minutes," said the mother.

Be prepared for challenges in the beginning of your marriage. They are a necessary to learn to grow together. When they occur, you cannot say to yourself, "I must have married the wrong person," or "This is not worth it." Work through challenges, no matter how they present themselves. Something positive can always be achieved through enduring hardships.

Change

Q: I get tired of my wife telling me that our problems would be solved if I would just "be the man she married." I try my best and get shot down by her, regardless of my efforts. It's discouraging because I feel the problem is all mine. What can I do to help her see that maybe she needs to change just as much as she thinks I need to?

Q: If I were to scale my marriage satisfaction, with one the lowest and ten the highest, I would say a five. When I realized this during a conference on marriage that my spouse and I attended, I got scared. There must be things that both of us can do to be more satisfied, but how do we start to change and then keep the changes we make permanent instead of relapsing into our old habits?

Q: My wife promised me that before we were married, she would change some of her destructive habits that made both of us unhappy. I don't feel that after six months of marriage Wendy is changing fast enough, and I realize that I can't live with some of the habits that have not yet been corrected. I am very close to giving up all hope that she will ever change. If she hasn't changed by now, I don't believe she ever will. How do I rekindle my belief in her when I see little evidence of change?

I've heard individuals say, "I'm the way I am, don't try to change me, I'm locked into it. If God wanted me different, He would have made me different." This type of philosophy is extremely detrimental to any marriage. The individual is really saying, "If there are differences, change over to my way; I won't (can't) change." It is important that people believe they have the ability to change or modify any behavior or characteristic about themselves that is irritating to others.

What is change? It is the shift from what is familiar to an area that is unfamiliar. Everyone likes to be comfortable and pain-free. Yet, the old adage, "no pain, no gain," applies to a marriage relationship. Change in marriage is undertaken because of our basic commitment to our spouse. In other words, if something we say, do, or believe is offensive to our partner, then changing ourself becomes the first area to look at. We cannot go around and change everyone that is different from us. We cannot blame others for our unhappiness.

I have seen individuals modify their temper, their priorities, and their personalities in order to make their spouse happier. Some blame the way they are on the theory of birth order, on parental upbringing (either positive or negative), or on their past. My opinion is that the past has an influence, but it does not have to determine our current behavior. Individuals need to learn from the past and not live in it. History doesn't have to determine destiny.

Why would an individual say, "I am the way I am?" For one reason, this attitude implies that they are not responsible for their personality or temperament. They don't understand that with God's help, all things are possible.

Individuals and married couples always compare themselves to others, believing that others are doing so much better than they are. Even though this thinking process might seem illogical and unworthy of emphasis, in marriage it is crucial not to compare. Rather, the person should focus on himself and on doing the very best he can to improve his imperfections. When we compare ourselves to others, we are comparing our weaknesses to their strengths and we will always come up short.

Just thinking about changing and having the strongest desires and intentions won't automatically translate into behavioral improvements. There has to be actions. Dreaming about what we want won't automatically make it happen. A lot of hard work, along with our dreaming, usually works together for our betterment. Focusing on how we can accomplish something is more productive than focusing solely on the negative, or why we can't do it.

We focus too much on how many imperfections we have, or on our spouse's imperfections, rather than on what we are doing to contribute to the problem. You as a couple should be concerned about growth, improvement, and change. It's all about choices. The following poem illustrates the point that there are two sides to every situation, and it is up to the individual to decide how he will deal with his circumstances.

THE TWO SIDES OF IT

There was a girl who always said
Her fate was very hard;
From the one thing she wanted most
She always was debarred.
There always was a cloudy spot
Somewhere within her sky;
Nothing was ever just quite right,
She used to say and sigh.

And yet her sister, strange to say,
Whose lot was quite the same,
Found something pleasant for herself
In every day that came.
Of course, things tangled up sometimes
For just a little while,
But nothing ever stayed all wrong,
She used to say and smile.

So one girl sighed and one girl smiled
Through all their lives together;
It didn't come from luck or fate,
From clear or cloudy weather.
The reason lay within their hearts
And colored all outside;
One chose to hope, and one to mope,
And so they smiled and sighed.[1]

—Anonymous—

Individuals are not justified in rationalizing their behavior by saying they can't change. It is my desire to provide hope, ownership, and empowerment to an individual so that he has the ability and authority to change his thinking and behavior.

HOW DOES CHANGE BEST OCCUR?

We shouldn't wait until we feel like making a change before we began. I hear people say, "I will make the necessary changes when I feel like doing them." They could be waiting a long time. Actions need to be taken, even when we don't feel like it. Over time, the feelings will come, even though they may not be present at first.

An obvious but unheeded bit of information is that we cannot change others; we can only change ourselves. No one wants to be changed against his will. But even when an individual wants his partner to change, and that partner does not want to change, all is not lost. By changing one element, the entire system can be affected. One person can make corrections or alterations that will impact the relationship. When you want someone to change, you usually have to acknowledge it by pointing out how they will benefit from making such a change, and the constructive impact it would have on you and the relationship. It is my hope that the sensitive, positive, and caring feelings that exist in relationships will be sufficient to motivate any necessary change.

There has to be an internal shift first—a change of attitude and feelings. There also has to be a softening of one's heart. When these internal changes have occurred, then the individual will make the necessary adjustments.

Now is the time to make any changes that need to be made; rationalizations need to be done away with and remorse needs to take their place. We need to bring our behavior up to our ideal level, rather than lowering our ideals to match our behavior.

Most people know what they need to do in order to make their marriage better. If that is a correct assumption, why don't they just do it? Why do they delay doing the right thing? If arrogance or self-importance are issues, remember that meekness and submissiveness are the necessary antidotes.

Some individuals might delay making their marriage better because their partner has not provided them with the proper incentives, or possibly because some minor differences or grudges are being held. For whatever reason, the counsel of Mother Teresa should help us all focus on why we are doing what we are doing.

DO IT ANYWAY

People are often unreasonable, illogical
And self-centered;
Forgive them anyway.

If you are kind, people may accuse you
Of selfish, ulterior motives;
Be kind anyway.

If you are successful, you will win some
False friends and some true enemies;
Succeed anyway.

If you are honest and frank,
People may cheat you;
Be honest and frank anyway.

If you spend years building, someone
Could destroy overnight;
Build anyway.

If you find serenity and happiness,
People may be jealous;
Be happy anyway.

The good you do today,
People will often forget tomorrow;
Do good anyway.

Give the world the best you have,
And it may never be enough;
Give the world the best you've got anyway.

You see, in the final analysis,
It is between you and God;
It was never between you and them anyway.[2]

—Mother Teresa—

In other words, don't let others and their reactions determine your behavior. We all need to be proactive in doing the right thing, simply because it is the right thing to do, even though others may cause some reason for us to reflect upon our intentions and behaviors.

Because we have the ability to analyze ourselves, our personalities, and our behaviors, we are not locked into set behaviors; we have the ability to change.

Empowering ourselves to make the necessary changes in a marriage relationship has far-reaching effects. Each of us, with restraint and effort, has the ability to control our thoughts and our behaviors. Do not delay in beginning this important voyage.

Notes

1. *The Children's Friend* (Salt Lake City: Deseret News, 1909), 245. (Digitized Nov. 26, 2007, Harvard University).

2. Mother Teresa, "Do it Anyway," www.geocities.com.

Cohabitation

Q: My boyfriend and I have been talking about moving in together. We plan on eventually getting married, but we want to make sure we will be able to make our relationship last. Both my parents and his parents got divorced, and neither of us wants to make the same mistakes our parents made. Why get married if we feel we can have many of the benefits of marriage even though we will be cohabiting? What information do you have that will help us decide whether we should just move in together or get married?

Since marriage is such a significant decision to make, it seems logical that living together for a period of time, to see if you are compatible with each other, would be the best choice. After all, how will you know if you will be right for each other unless you have a trial run? Cohabitation usually means two people verbally agree to live together, sharing sex, meals, apartment, and some time. For some, cohabitation is a positive experience. Being married means the same thing, except that the couple has made promises to stay together through the hard times, as well as the good times.

As logical as living together before marrying seems, research and comments made by church leaders of any denomination speak contrary to living together prior to marriage.

Even though there are many answers why this might be the case, there is one major reason living together prior to marriage does not work. It has to do with commitment. There is no commitment or lasting bond present to keep this relationship in existence.

Additionally, cohabiting partners are living together on a trial basis and are waiting to see if their needs will be met by the other individual. If individual needs are not met by their partner, there is no commitment between them and it becomes easier to bail out rather than work through differences. The main focus is, "Will you meet my needs?" rather than, "Can I meet your needs?" It's more of a taking rather than giving type of relationship. For this reason, each partner makes little investment. That is most often translated into one of the partners feeling devalued because of the lack of giving on the part of the other partner.

In the majority of cases, cohabitation does not lead to marriage. Among cohabitants who do marry, their chances of divorce are actually increased. No one has ever proven that cohabitation makes a positive contribution to marital stability.

One of the most comprehensive articles written about cohabitation is by Jeffry H. Larson, a professor of marriage and family therapy at Brigham Young University. The article, "The Verdict on Cohabitation vs. Marriage," includes an extensive and thorough bibliography with sources that confirm the dangers of cohabitation. I encourage you to read the article in its entirety, but will quote here some of Larson's major conclusions to help support the notion that marriage, in all ways, is far superior to cohabitation:

> Research from the last 30 years shows that living together before marriage doesn't increase satisfaction or stability in marriage. "Compared to marriage, cohabitation creates disadvantages for individuals, couples, and children." Cohabitation can increase a couple's chances of divorce for several reasons. Those who choose to live together are often more unconventional than others and tend to be less committed to marriage as an institution. Or they may be people who are afraid of commitment and permanence or who believe from observation that marriage can't last. . . .

> Second, cohabitants may value independence more than non-cohabitants and are less likely than married people to support or be financially responsible for their partners. They may have separate bank accounts. Finally, cohabitants may have negative attitudes about marriage and see divorce as a solution to marriage problems. In contrast, the long-term contract of marriage encourages emotional investment in the relationship and sexual fidelity. Marriage contributes to healthy emotional development of children and efforts to protect financial status by monitoring each other's spending and planning together.

There is less aggression and abuse in marriages, and married men make more money than single men.[1]

Notes

1. Jeffry H. Larson, "The Verdict on Cohabitation vs. Marriage," *Marriage & Families*, Jan., 7-12, 2001, 31, http://marriageandfamilies.byu.edu/issues/2001/January/cohabitation.htm.

Commitment

Q: With today's high divorce rate, I am afraid of getting married because of the total commitment that is needed to make marriage successful. I don't think I am ready for all the changes that marriage will cause in my life. How can I overcome my fear of marriage and make such a commitment to another person?

There is an underlying question being asked: "Is there any way to guarantee a successful marriage?" The obvious answer is no. Many programs and premarital tests claim an extremely high prediction rate for couples contemplating marriage, but there is not a 100 percent guarantee.

Another underlying question is, "Am I ready to put someone else's needs before my own?" This might be referred to as "growing up."

Also behind the question is the fear of failure. No one wants to enter into a marriage thinking there might be close to a 50 percent chance of this relationship failing.

A recent study conducted by prominent social scientists David Popenoe and Barbara Defoe Whitehead found that "young people in the United States today are increasingly apprehensive and pessimistic about marriage. They display a remarkable increase in acceptance of out-of-wedlock childbearing, single parenting, and living together before marriage. No wonder the number of people getting married in the United States has dropped so markedly."[1]

There is a delightful poem that illustrates what a couple might look like if they put off marrying for too long.

TO HAVE AND TOO OLD

The bride, white of hair, is stooped over her cane
Her faltering footsteps need guiding,
While down the church aisle, with wan toothless smile,
The groom in a wheelchair comes riding.
And who is this elderly couple you ask?
You'll find when you've closely explored it,
That here is that rare, most conservative pair,
Who waited 'til they could afford it.[2]

—Richard Armour—

Over the past years the average marriage age has increased. People in their twenties have a lot of pressure on them to complete school and prepare for the future. Getting married is a priority too, but when that occurs is not ironclad; it can be postponed until other "essentials" in a person's life occur.

No one should rush into making this very important decision. However, if the delay is caused by fear of failure, lack of confidence, or unresolved past issues, action should be taken to confront those issues and the pursuit of dating and finding a potential marriage partner should take more of their time.

Q: Being married has been a little different than I imagined. It was so much fun to be married at first, but most of that excitement has left with time. I thought my wife and I were so compatible, but now I am not so sure. I am thinking that if I left my wife I could find someone who would better meet my needs. What are my chances of this actually happening?

A basic ingredient needed for any successful marriage is that of commitment. A commitment to the marriage can't be shallow or superficial. It is not just a convenience or a one-time event. Rather, it is a vital, ongoing process that needs to be renewed on a regular basis. This commitment means that there will be no other significant person in a couple's life like that of their spouse. There can be friends, business associates, and even passing fantasies (such as a movie star). However, these individuals should not be a permanent part of your life's plan.

At the beginning of your relationship, determine the level of your commitment to each other. Even after making a firm commitment, you should realize that there will be moments of despair and discouragement and yes, even at times, unhappiness. However, a strong commitment to each other can bring about a permanent change when necessary.

Q: My husband and I have been married for seventeen years. We've made it through some rough times, but he doesn't want to be married anymore. He says the relationship is not satisfying to him and he is not as committed as he used to be, and knows he should feel more committed. I am not ready to give up on our relationship, our family, and everything we've built together. What suggestions do you have for me—especially when one of us wants to make this marriage work and the other wants to throw in the towel?

Commitment is a choice to make your marriage work. This commitment has to be physical, emotional, psychological, and spiritual. If a couple expects their original flame to be just as bright after ten, twenty, or thirty years of marriage, without effort on their part, they might be headed for trouble. This, in part, might be a reason some individuals seek love outside the marriage relationship. It is important that the couple keep the door tightly shut on any outside relationships. Don't let yourself even think about other possibilities. I believe that if the marriage was right in the first place, the flame may be out, but the embers are still glowing and with some effort and commitment from both partners, the flame can burn again. Be committed to each other and focus on meeting each other's needs.

Commitment is a major factor in strong marriages. Determination, a proper attitude, and skill development must also exist. I'm disappointed that marriage vows do not seem to be taken seriously among many couples.

There are three types of commitment:

1. **Personal commitment**. This is the best form of commitment; it is voluntary and doesn't involve pressure. The individual wants to stay in the marriage because of the benefits, love, and obligations that they are willing to be a part of. The commitment that was made at the beginning of the relationship is still in force.

2. **Moral commitment**. This has to do with an individual's feeling that he should stay in the relationship. Even though some

personal needs are not being met, he feels a moral obligation and responsibility to continue.

3. **Structural commitment**. The individual feels he has to stay in the relationship because of the children, finances, health insurance, and living arrangements. With this type of commitment, there is usually resentment and bitterness because the individual feels locked in.

COVENANT RELATIONSHIPS

Marriage and family ties involve covenant relationships. These are serious promises that have been made, and they cannot be regarded lightly. With divorce rates escalating throughout the world, it is apparent that many spouses are failing to endure in their covenants to honor and sustain each other. A couple committed to each other does not have to be perfect; they are only required to work together toward an improved relationship.

I once worked with a couple who had been married for three months. When asked what the problem was, the wife replied by saying that when they first got married, her husband promised that he would not watch TV on Sunday, but he did it anyway—every week. Her conclusion was, "If he'll lie to me about this, he'll lie to me about other things. I want out of the marriage now before it gets worse."

I was very concerned about the level of commitment this wife had to her marriage. I am not judging whether the husband should or should not watch TV on Sunday. Rather, because of that behavior, she was making a decision that preempted her married commitments. I tried in vain to help her look at other aspects of the marriage, but her husband's behavior overshadowed any good that might have existed.

Decide now to recommit yourself to your spouse. If you do, your marriage will become energized through your newfound desire to serve your spouse.

Notes

1. K. Hamilton and P. Wingert, "Down the Aisle," *Newsweek*, 20 July 1998, 54–57.

2. Richard Willard Armour, *Light Armour: Playful Poems on Practically Everything* (New York: McGraw Hill, 1954), 5.

Communication

Q: Kelsey and I need some help with our communication. We once talked openly about nearly every subject, but lately it seems like all we ever discuss are children and bills. I feel like our relationship is losing some of its steam because our conversations are limited to the same topics all the time. When we do try to communicate, we usually say many things that are attacking and hurtful. How can we improve our communication and become closer to one another?

Q: Many of the disagreements my husband, Bill, and I have could be avoided if we talked about things earlier on. For example, I learned last week that Bill thinks I've been spending too much time working at our son's elementary school. I think he is jealous of the time I spend with my son. I can't read his mind! When he has these problems, I wish he would come out and tell me what is bothering him. However, when Bill tells me what's bothering him, I often leave with hurt feelings and then I am unable to talk with him about the problems I am having. Can you help us with our communication dilemma?

There will be some who read the title of this chapter and skip over it. They say to themselves, "I know how to speak, I can talk with other people, and I don't need to learn more." There is, however, more to communication than mere talking. How we talk, the words we use, precipitating events, the emotional state of the parties involved, and how our words are perceived by others are all necessary ingredients in effective communication.

Still, others will read the title of this chapter and think that the importance of communication in marriage is overemphasized.

The purpose of this chapter is not to introduce communication styles, programs, techniques, or workshop-oriented materials. The purpose is to present principles and doctrines related to communication. You can then make whatever adjustments necessary in your own life.

Words Can Inflict Pain

A husband might never think of beating his wife physically, but might on occasion use words that belittle or demean her. Words can convey love and caring, or they can convey hate and anger. The words we use are influenced by many factors.

Intentional vs. Unintentional

Since we are all human, we all make mistakes. There have been times in our lives when we have communicated inappropriately, either intentionally or unintentionally. I am confident that each of us has inflicted pain in the lives of loved ones because of our words. I would hope, however, that no one would be guilty of intentionally hurting, belittling, or inflicting pain on another.

Communication Is More than Words

To have effective communication in a marriage, a sincere feeling of caring for the other must be present and perceived by both spouses. This is probably the single most important quality in improving personal, in-depth communication. Some couples say, "We just can't communicate, so why even try? It's no use." These couples are really saying that for some reason they can't discuss meaningful emotional issues with their partner, yet they desire to.

It is impossible not to communicate. Everything we do is a form of communication, and when we choose not to communicate, we are still communicating—just in a different manner. When we know someone cares for us, we are more likely to open up and share personal information with him. Remember, communication is not just talking, it is "sharing of oneself totally." Both partners have a responsibility to make the atmosphere psychologically safe so that effective communication and the sharing of personal feelings will continue.

Using Absolutes

Each of us can remember a time when someone has said, "you never," or "you always." How did those remarks make you feel? Human beings, for the most part, don't "always" or "never" do something. By virtue of being human, we respond to our emotions, feelings, and behaviors. We are not absolute beings. Yes, there are times when we can be consistent, but it usually bothers us when someone tells us that we *always* say or do something, or that we *never* say or do something.

In a counseling session, a wife mentioned to her husband, "You never tell me that you love me." He replied, "Of course I do, I just don't tell you as much as you would like." This case illustrates the "all or nothing" principle. When most of us do not get what we want, we don't say, "I would like a little more." Rather, we negatively personalize our expectations and needs not being met, turning it into a catastrophic event. We then say to our partner, "you never," or "you always." What the wife was really trying to say was, "I know you love me, but it is important for me to hear you say it more than you do now." To this, the husband could more easily respond, "I'll try and work on that because it's important to you, but be patient with me in the process."

The words *always* or *never* usually negate all the attempts and efforts of the offended person. It gives him an excuse (albeit lame) to stop trying, since his efforts are not recognized at all. Over time, he builds resentment toward the person who does not recognize his effort.

Q: My wife, Emily, has always been very active. She has a whirlwind personality, and that is one of the qualities that first attracted me to her. Emily is involved with our children, is very busy with the PTA and other school functions, is a volunteer in some community groups, and is currently serving as a member of the city council. I sometimes feel jealous and resentful. Emily doesn't seem to devote much time to our relationship anymore. Every time I start to talk about this situation, she becomes upset, and we aren't able to communicate our concerns. We both feel like we are unable to keep up with everything going on in our lives, *and* make the necessary time to communicate with each other.

Guidelines to Improve Communication

Feelings not talked out have to be acted out. It ought to be a clue to Emily's husband that when he starts to talk about his feelings, she becomes upset. He needs to ask himself, "Why do I get so upset?" My hunch is that he holds in a lot of resentment toward Emily because of the time she spends away from home and not with him, or that when he begins to talk, he attacks her and blames her for his feelings. When Emily feels attacked, she retaliates. With this cycle, nothing is accomplished. The focus needs to be on stating feelings without attacking the other person; focus on the problem, not a symptom of the problem. How is this accomplished?

1. Be in control before any discussion is commenced.
2. Be aware of the feelings that are being experienced.
3. Be able to state these feelings in the form of an "I" message.

"I" messages consist of the emotion being felt, along with the behavior of the other person. For example, "I feel [emotion] when you [behavior]." Notice that there is no attacking or rationalizing, but rather a basic statement. It is not saying that the other person caused your feeling, but rather the perception that created the feelings. The only recourse the other person could have with this statement is, "You shouldn't feel the way you do." The response would be, "Maybe I shouldn't, but I do." Don't try and talk yourself out of the feeling or rationalize it. At this point, your job is to merely express it.

The mere expression of feelings does not guarantee a change in the other person's behavior. It is important to express a desire of how the person would like the situation to be. If the other individual can accommodate the expectation, then the problem is resolved.

Important aspects of communication include the following:

- Learn to listen.
- Be specific and reasonable in your requests.
- Use positive and corrective feedback.
- Clarify what you mean as you give messages.
- Learn to ask questions.

For couples to be effective in their communication, they need to learn to do four simple things:

1. Plan in their minds first what they are going to say.
2. Express their feelings succinctly.
3. Don't use absolutes.
4. Speak softly.

Q: Betty gets her feelings hurt almost daily by her spouse and by other people in her life. She seems to constantly be on the defensive. She doesn't feel like her husband will listen to her concerns and that he may even get angry if she were to bring them up. Every time she and her husband argue, Betty says it is impossible to win, so she doesn't even try. Instead, she keeps her resentful and hurt feelings inside.

It would be easy to say that Betty's husband has a problem. We will focus on him later, but first, let's focus on Betty. Betty needs to take inventory of herself first. Some questions she might ask are: "How often do I state my concerns to my husband?" and "Why am I constantly on the defense?"

Focus on the Self First

When couples face differences in their marriage, they must focus first on the self. We cannot go around trying to change other people to meet our needs and fit our expectations. In the above scenario, the husband would say that the wife is always talking and wants him to listen no matter what. Intellectually, he wants to listen to her. But regardless of what happens, both just end up being offended. Betty could make sure that she is not talking to her husband only about her concerns, but also about the positive aspects of her life. She could also invite her husband to share his feelings and thoughts. There is a possibility that she might be bringing up too much too often and expecting all her questions to be answered immediately. The constant barrage could put him on overload. She could make sure that she chooses to discuss issues with her husband at a time that is convenient for him too.

Betty's husband needs to do all he can to anticipate how she will respond to him. It would be easy to just say, "Well, that's her problem." He needs to be more concerned about her comfort and well-being than he is about his own.

Q: I have been married for twenty-two years, and I believe it's about time my husband knew what I wanted and needed without me having to tell him all the time. Frankly, I don't feel comfortable coming right out and telling him, because if he does what I ask, it will be because I asked him to, and not because he thought about it first and wanted to. I'm not asking him to read my mind, but after so many years of married life, I would think certain things would be common sense to him.

The myth of this scenario is, "If you love me, you will know what I'm thinking, feeling, and what my needs are." The only way a marriage partner knows what his spouse wants is for her to put her thoughts and desires into words. No one can read minds. We can guess and speculate, and the longer we live together, the more accurate we may become. However, the only true way to know what's going on in your partner's mind is to ask.

COMMUNICATION CYCLE

If we don't communicate accurately because our feelings have been hurt, we begin to build negative emotions within ourselves. We then withhold, withdraw, and disengage from the other person. The different levels of our communication can help us become better communicators.

LEVELS OF COMMUNICATION

Communication can be divided into three categories: superficial, personal, and validation.

1. **Superficial**—Topics in this category are easy to discuss with anyone. This involves non-risky topics such as weather, sports, cars, school, church, movies, house, or jobs. There is little investment of self or personal risk. There is not much investment of thought or worry about outcome.

2. **Personal**—This category involves a level of communication that brings out our personal opinions, ideas, values, thoughts, and feelings. There is more risk involved because we are never sure how others will react to our ideas, feelings, and thoughts. We are very sensitive to how others react when we share at this level. If someone disagrees or has a different opinion than we do, we usually revert back to a superficial level, a safer level, or a nonconfrontational level.

3. **Validation**—This level of communication conveys positive messages of appreciation, love, respect, and gratitude. It usually indicates the value or worth of another to you. The communication may be verbal or nonverbal (touch, wink, compliment), but it must be positive. There is more risk involved, which implies a

higher risk of possible rejection. Validation, if used too much, can be misconstrued as phony or manipulative.

Communication at the validation level is risky for the person providing the validation. Remember not to discount a compliment (validation) or a positive accolade someone extends to you. If a person says you look nice, or gave a good talk, sometimes you may discount his gesture by saying, "This is an old shirt," or "I didn't do my best because I couldn't read my notes." The person paying you a compliment should feel better after having given you the validation than before it was given. All you need to say is, "Thank you very much; that means a lot to me."

Summary Points

When we communicate with our spouse and children at the personal and validating levels of communication, we meet their needs *and* our needs. We meet the need to feel loved, valued, accepted, and appreciated. Trust develops because we have confidence in each other that we can share our heartfelt thoughts and feelings without being laughed at, rejected, or put down. In meeting these personal needs through others, we generate emotions.

We cannot throw out the superficial level, however, because it is essential to process information, begin a relationship, convey ideas, and converse normally with others. Without this level, we could not function very well in interpersonal exchanges.

In strained, tense marriages or parent/child relationships, of course, communication must be superficial because it is the only safe level that can be used without creating emotional displays. If feelings are fragile, it may be difficult to communicate even at the superficial level.

But the superficial level does not meet personal needs or convey positive messages (validation). Therefore, we do not want to remain at this level in any relationship.

Listening

Listening is an act of love. Individuals communicate with their entire body—eyes, ears, arms, face. This is called body language. As important as this is, we must keep in mind that 80 percent of communication is listening. Listening is important for three major reasons:

1. We listen to understand.

2. Understanding is more important than agreeing.
3. Understanding is a large part of loving.

On Listening

The following two lists are modified from original lists contributed by The Bloemfontein Samaritans in South Africa.

You are listening to me when you do the following:

- You come quietly into my private world and let me be me.
- You really try to understand me, even if I'm not making much sense.
- You grasp my point of view, even when it's against your own sincere convictions.
- You allow me the dignity of making my own decisions even though you think they might be wrong.
- You do not take my problem from me but allow me to deal with it in my own way.
- You hold back your desire to give me good advice.
- You give me enough room to discover for myself what is really going on.
- You accept my gift of gratitude by telling me how good it makes you feel to know you have been helpful.

You are not listening to me when you do the following:

- You say you understand before you know me well enough.
- You have an answer for my problem before I've finished telling you what my problem is.
- You cut me off before I finish speaking.
- You finish my sentence for me.
- You are critical of my vocabulary, grammar, or accent.
- You tell me about your experience, making mine seem unimportant.
- You are communicating to someone else in the room.
- You refuse my thanks by saying you haven't really done anything.[1]

The Virtue of Silence

There is a difference between listening and silence. As just described, listening with every part of your being is a major element of effective communication. At other times, another person will say something that will press a button and you will become silent, just waiting for your opportunity to retaliate.

Effective Communication

Listed below are excuses I have heard individuals use to rationalize their ineffective communication style:

1. Inherited from family of origin. In some homes, good communication is not modeled or taught, and one simply doesn't know how to communicate.
2. Birth order can also play a factor in one's communication style. The oldest child is usually a high achiever, bright, and so forth. The second child may not be as bright, is a follower, and is more of a peacemaker. The third child is typically manipulative and undercuts others.
3. Lazy—don't want to put forth the effort.
4. Worried about getting hurt.
5. Don't know the difference between talking and communicating.
6. Use the excuse that God made them that way.

Communication Myths

Often, individuals don't communicate because of some previously held myths. Below I have summarized some myths that I have heard over the years. They are:

1. Actions speak louder than words; therefore, actions are more important than words.
2. In most marriages where there are problems, couples do not communicate.
3. Stating your problems always builds the marriage relationship.
4. If you love me, you'll know what I'm thinking, feeling, and what my needs are.
5. The more open and honest the communication, the better the relationship.
6. If a spouse doesn't state feelings, it means he doesn't have any.
7. Those who talk the most in a relationship have the most power or control.

8. To refuse to talk when angry or upset is always a cop-out.

9. When communicating, always focus on the other person, rather than yourself.

10. Yelling is a good way to communicate; it releases the suppressed feelings.

COMMUNICATING FRUSTRATION

It is imperative that a couple learn how to effectively communicate frustration, disappointment, irritation, and anger. Before a person speaks, he needs to first think through the emotions he is experiencing: What triggered the emotion? What were the dynamics of feeling this way? What were the perceptions of the event that caused the emotion? It is not helpful to constantly suppress these emotions. Suppressed resentment and anger begins to simmer and cause bitterness toward another person (the perceived source causing one's negative emotions), which then leads to further complications.

The best way to deal with anger is to identify the source of it and calmly discuss it with your partner. Do not attack or blame; rather, merely express the emotion you are experiencing. It would be helpful to say, "I'm feeling upset . . ." You cannot deny the emotion, and to say that you are not experiencing the emotion is not realistic. Avoiding effective communication is a major contributor to unhappy marriages.

Notes

1. Ralph Roughton, "Introduction To Basic Listening Skills Activity," www.itslifejimbutnotasweknowit.org. (List contributed by the Bloemfontein Samaritans in South Africa.)

Criticism

Q: My spouse's faults were minimal when we were newly married, but now they are looming and many. I am almost constantly criticizing, especially over the little things that should not matter. What is the difference, and what is my problem? How can I let go of the things that should be insignificant but are driving me crazy?

Q: Barbara has always had a joking personality. She enjoys playing practical jokes and has hundreds of stories about the pranks she played when she was in high school and college. She also has a great sense of humor. When Barbara and her husband, Bill, go to parties, Barbara is often the center of attention, telling hilarious stories that have the whole room in stitches. She seems to be able to find a joke about nearly everything, although sometimes her jokes are at the expense of others. Bill has been the brunt of several of Barbara's jokes, but she always just tells him she's kidding and gives Bill a hug afterward. Bill has found that several of Barbara's jokes are very hurtful and seem more like criticism. Bill told Barbara that some of the things she jokes about really hurt him. If this was the story of your marriage, what would you do about it?

Sometimes individuals are so caught up in making a good impression, being the life of the party, or trying to positively influence other people that they become less sensitive to the reactions of the person who is the brunt of their jokes. If the person who is the brunt of someone's jokes tries to approach that individual about his feelings, he will usually be thought of as overreacting, or being too sensitive.

Love should provide us with the desire to want our spouse to be happy. When we make comments that hurt our spouse, he may perceive and personalize our comments as meaning, "I don't care about your feelings. I don't love you." No matter how strong our love once was, over the years, repeated criticism of our spouse can cause contention in our relationship.

If you really love your spouse, you will care so much for his happiness that you will not say anything to diminish it. Before you say anything, you must always ask yourself, "What impact will my comments have on my spouse?" In other words, you need to edit what you're going to say before it is said. If there is even a question in your mind that what you say will have a negative impact, you shouldn't say it. All verbal expressions toward your spouse should be filled with praise, admiration, and gentleness.

It's your choice. You can spend your life criticizing your spouse, defending your rights, protecting your ego, pointing out mistakes, uncovering faults, and letting him know your irritation. But if you choose this course, you will find that your spouse's love for you will be badly tarnished. You will notice that the criticism you have leveled toward him will have taken a toll.

Of course, you can make a wiser choice. You can expend the effort to change yourself so your words continually reflect your profound love and respect.

As married partners, you and your spouse need to feel comfortable with the notion, "We're not yet perfect, but we're both still trying." You need to allow each other a chance to improve and progress. Demanding instant perfection of your partner isn't realistic. It's practical for you to seriously work to improve and perfect yourself and to also lovingly assist your partner when and how you can—but do it at his invitation.

There is no place in a loving marriage relationship for criticism and faultfinding. If there are issues that need to be altered, certainly there are more effective ways than criticizing or putting down your spouse. It has been generally accepted that the faults we find in others are usually those faults that we have ourselves. Before criticizing your spouse, look in the mirror and discover the fault you're projecting onto your spouse.

Differences

Q: My wife and I have so many differences. We're newlyweds, but we don't see eye to eye on many subjects. I sometimes wonder if our decision to marry was truly a wise choice. I never dreamed there would be so many areas where our individual families have done things so differently. I can see that we'll need to compromise in several areas. Because marriage is important to us, what can we do to best resolve our differences and compromise?

Q: When Jed and I disagree, he pulls out all the stops and tells me everything that has been bothering him in the past month. I love my spouse, but when he does this, he gets on my nerves. I try to overlook this annoying aspect of our relationship, but it's hard. He'll bring up all the mistakes I have made previously and throw them in my face. Jed says he can't stand keeping all these emotions inside and that it's unhealthy for me to keep everything bottled up all the time. During an argument, is it really healthy to get it out of your system no matter what you have to say? If not, what is a more healthy way to resolve conflicts?

Q: My wife and I hardly agree on anything. Every time we talk, we end up in a big fight that lasts for days. Sometimes we argue over things that I know we will never agree on. When we disagree, she says I have to show my love for her by letting her have her way. Is this right?

Differences in marriage are universal and are an essential part of lives. Just think for a moment of how many billions of people have lived upon the earth. Now think of how many of those people are identical in every facet of their lives: appearance, mannerisms, morals, likes, and dislikes. The answer is a staggering zero. Nobody is identical to anyone else in every aspect of his life. Marrying someone who thinks and acts identically as you is impossible. Therefore, differences in a marriage are inevitable. The question that naturally arises for any couple is, "What are you going to focus more on in your marriage, the similarities or the differences?"

Every marriage has differences. They're inevitable. If a couple says they don't have differences or disagreements in their marriage, they're either not telling the truth, or they are old and have forgotten all past disagreements. If indeed they do have such a marriage, they are the envy of everyone who knows them.

Resolving conflict, while sometimes painful, is a healthy part of living that can build faith, fortitude, and character. However, if conflict is left unresolved, it can lead to contention and disputation.

Differences don't mean that one spouse has to be right and the other wrong or that one opinion is better than the other; nor do they mean that every issue has to be resolved. In fact, some couples have to learn to live with the reality that certain differences will never be resolved, and they must simply agree to disagree.

One of the greatest blessings to any marriage is the opportunity to share and obtain other viewpoints and feelings on the various issues that arise. This needs to be done in a manner that is supportive rather than destructive to the relationship, and that allows couples to develop skills that will turn their differences into opportunities.

In resolving marital conflicts, remember that this is a continual process that should never be taken for granted. It is essential for a couple to discover that real peace and contentment can come as both develop the sensitivity and the skills needed to resolve differences when conflicts arise. Couples will need to continue to work hard and put forth the necessary effort so the marriage relationship will improve each day. The skill of conflict management can be acquired with some time and effort.

WHY DIFFERENCES IN MARRIAGE

In marriage, the opportunity for diversity is greater because of the closeness of the relationship. Contrasts exist because in any intimate relationship, there are two unique individuals with different backgrounds, thoughts, and opinions. Differences between spouses are merely a result of the uniqueness and characteristics of each individual. In order to achieve success in marriage, each partner must be willing to give and take, and to occasionally alter personal views and opinions for the good of the marriage. This is particularly important in areas where discord has a negative effect, causes conflict, or is destructive to the relationship.

Differences in a relationship do not mean that the marriage is destined to be unsuccessful; they don't need to damage the relationship. Differences should not be viewed as the foundation of marriage; instead, they can be a great strength. Good marriages are not made in heaven. They must be constantly nurtured.

Disagreements do not need to escalate to conflict, then anger, then rage. From my experience as a therapist, I have found that couples will always disagree about certain things; yet, there are some issues that, when discussed, might be modified.

UNDERSTANDING DIFFERENCES

How can two apparently well-adjusted individuals marry each other, only to have the marriage turn into a negative relationship? In marriage relationships, we are required to be concerned for the feelings, desires, wants, needs, comforts, and attitudes of someone else more than we are concerned for our own.

For a moment, let's be honest with ourselves. To some degree, we all say, "If there were more people in the world like me, it would be a better place." We think this because we believe we have it all together. We know we aren't perfect, but we say to ourselves, "Just look at me. I'm okay, I've handled life just fine." This self-talk might be modified somewhat, but the message is usually the same. If I were talking to you and we discovered a difference between us, my first impulse would be to think, "Well, I know who's right and who's wrong." We believe that others ought to agree with our way of thinking. If they don't, they're wrong. By having this mind-set, we fail to see how our actions and attitudes contribute to conflict. As long as I believe you're the one who needs to change and you believe that I'm the one who needs to change, we'll find ourselves in a stalemate. Instead of looking at myself and asking what I can do to resolve the conflict, I spend most of my energy trying to persuade you to my way of thinking, which becomes exhausting and detrimental to our relationship.

THE GOAL OF DIFFERENCES

The first goal in helping a couple deal effectively with their differences is to get them to work on the self, and not try to change the partner. "The goal in marriage is not to think alike, but to think together."[1]

Another goal is to realize that not all conflicts will be resolved. It's wishful thinking to believe otherwise, because one partner would have to give up a core belief or value, and that sacrifice would be too much to ask. When a difference is discovered, pressure is applied to the spouse to change his viewpoint to agree with yours. We do not need to change everyone we meet in life to our way of thinking. How ridiculous to believe that, especially of your spouse.

Why is so much time spent trying to change others? People feel powerful, important, and in control when they successfully alter an external situation or change another's attitude or behavior. Some conflicts will just have to be tolerated. Most of us believe that all differences have to be resolved if the marriage is going to succeed. This is not the case.

A major problem arises when differences are personalized and you feel rejected by your partner for not changing to your way of thinking. When a spouse feels attacked, he will personalize it, feeling hurt and most likely having the desire to strike back. Sometimes, a spouse will personalize any difference in the marriage and say, "You don't love me," or "It's always my fault." Or, he will have a pity party. These responses are usually done so the spouse can be rescued and reassured of his worth as a person. If this pattern is noticed between a couple, the focus needs to be shifted from the topic at hand to how personalizing differences and feeling sorry for yourself or playing the role of victim interferes with resolving differences.

There are many gimmicks and models of problem-solving; however, love, respect, and appreciation need to be present between a couple first, or it won't matter what model or technique is utilized—it will not be effective.

HOW DIFFERENCES AFFECT THE MARRIAGE RELATIONSHIP

Based on my experience in counseling couples and families, I have found that understanding and implementing the following principles will help couples better deal with the inevitable disagreements in their marriages.

Differences are normal and essential for personal growth and couple cohesiveness. Marriage provides opportunities for differences to occur. They don't need to be viewed as negative, but rather as character-building. Problem-solving has a very constructive role to play in marriage—it compels us to develop effective ways of handling differences.

Differences in a marriage should be seen by a couple as an opportunities for growth—not as punishments. This awareness will have a positive impact on the relationship. Conversely, if a couple avoids dealing with conflict, they can slow their progress toward emotional intimacy. A certain amount of stress and dissatisfaction is normal and can occur from time to time, even in "good" relationships.

Many marriages present such a peaceful surface that you might think, "They never have any disagreements. What's wrong with our marriage?" That kind of comparison will not help you. We usually see others at their best and compare them to our worst. What we need as a model is a couple who knows how to resolve difficulties; in other words, we all need to see how others productively implement basic principles, skills, and attitudes to solve their challenges together.

Properly handling disagreements can make you more durable, more open to other adjustments, and less vulnerable to challenges to yourself, to your relationships, or to your family. Furthermore, actually tackling a challenge generates an immense amount of energy and builds confidence.

Differences are best resolved in an environment of mutual love, consideration, and respect. To be effective in dealing with disagreements in any relationship, especially marriage, you should have attributes such as patience, gentleness, selflessness, kindness, love, cooperation, respect, humility, forgiveness, understanding, courtesy, consideration, trust, and commitment. Couples who address problems in a spirit of love, compassion, and mutual respect will have greater success than those who are determined to achieve selfish interests. However, when serious arguments go unresolved, it is usually because one or both of the partners lack one of these attributes.

Conversely, traits that can cause contention in the marriage relationship would include being self-centered, prideful, stubborn, arrogant, selfish, judgmental, and intolerant. In my experience, couples experiencing the most difficulty demonstrate one or more of these traits.

At the risk of sounding simplistic, the root causes of marital conflict are self-importance and self-centeredness. These twin plagues make it difficult for a person to apologize, take responsibility for his own actions, and change himself and improve the relationship. A prideful, selfish individual can't believe (or doesn't want to believe) that he could be the source of the problem. The antidote to pride is humility.

A husband once told me, "To be honest, if my wife and I have a difference, it is usually her fault. I'm not perfect, but I can always show her where she initiated the problem. Sometimes I just don't understand why she feels a certain way on a specific subject."

One can only wonder how the wife felt about herself and toward her husband, who held this opinion as a core belief. In this example, the husband needs to realize he can state the emotions his wife experiences without experiencing the same emotions himself with the same intensity. This would go a long way to ease tensions and resolve differences.

SEPARATING THE PERSON FROM THE PROBLEM

In resolving disputes, a couple must be gentle and kind with each other. Calmly discussing problems —details, facts, timelines, outcomes— in the spirit of cooperation, respect, and love is vital to understanding each other. Accusing, blaming, labeling, or attacking each other is never helpful. What a person does is not who he is. It is very important to separate the content of the problem from the emotion; be soft on the person and tough on the problem.

The goal is to avoid attacking the person and to simply address the problem. Below are some examples of negative reactions to common marriage issues and the positive reactions that should be used instead:

- **Negative**: "If *you* would work harder and not be so lazy, we wouldn't be in the financial fix we're in."
- **Positive**: "What can *we* do to earn more money?"

- **Negative**: "If *you* didn't have to be right all the time, we would have a better relationship."
- **Positive**: "Let's talk about how *we* can have a better relationship."

I occasionally hear a husband respond to his wife by stating that a particular problem "is yours, not mine." Any difficulty in marriage affects both partners; thus, conflicts are best solved together. The focus should not be on *who's* right but on *what's* right. Differences are not necessarily a sign of the failure of the marriage or immoral living by one of the partners, but rather, an expression of the uniqueness that exists in each individual.

Emphasizing the Positive Aspects of Marriage

We all do better with compliments, especially from our spouse, even though it seems to be easier to point out our spouse's negative behaviors.

A marriage partner knows what to do to please the other, so why don't they just do it? One response to that question might include, "I don't feel like it." You can't wait until you feel like it—the behavior might never happen. Just start doing the right thing and the feeling will come. If it doesn't, at least you'll know you acted appropriately. Another response might be, "I don't want to, or I don't know how." You have the ability to respond to situations in life any way you choose. If you don't know how, learn. Ask for help. There is no excuse. If the goal is to be reached, the effort must be made.

John Gottman, a respected social science researcher, found that couples who stayed married emphasized the positive with each other more than the negative. In fact, for every negative interaction that occurs in a relationship, there needs to be at least five positive interactions to offset it.[2]

Some Differences Will Never Be Resolved

John Gottman found in his research that 69 percent of disagreements are over what he refers to as "perpetual problems."[3] These problems will never be resolved. In these instances, the couple needs to agree to disagree.

Gottman also found that 31 percent of disagreements are over problems that can be altered. These couples are happier than were the couples who focus on the perpetual problems.[4]

Effects of Ignoring Differences

Differences left unresolved can escalate from disagreements, to conflict, to contentions, to anger, and finally to rage. When emotions get out of control, reality can get distorted, and then efforts to resolve differences are not as effective. If a relationship is not based on mutual love, respect, trust, and caring, the implementation of any procedure to solve problems is of little effect.

SIMPLE PROBLEM TRIGGERS

The bottom line is that both you and your spouse have buttons that can be easily pushed. Once pushed, these buttons have the potential of creating great destruction within a marriage. It seems silly to make a fuss over such small issues. But aren't there times when you do? Do any of these potential conflict triggers exist in your marriage?

- The toothpaste tube squeezed incorrectly.
- Food not covered properly in the refrigerator.
- Towels left on the bathroom floor.
- Hair left on the bathroom counter and in the sink.
- Checks not logged in the check register.
- Clothes scattered throughout the house.
- Fingernail or toenail clippings left in the living room.
- An expensive item purchased without your spouse's knowledge.
- Trash left in car.
- Drinking directly from the milk container.

MYTHS

One of the biggest myths is that a happy marriage is a "difference-free" marriage. The goal should not be to eliminate all differences, but to minimize those you can and learn to cope with those you can't. Some conflicts occur in marriage because one of the partners believes in some long-standing myths from over the years. If you have differences in your marriage or family, you might think that you made a mistake by marrying your partner. A successful marriage is not derived from how much we are alike originally; it is a result of how many differences we can learn to tolerate and reconcile with each other.

A fulfilling marriage relationship doesn't happen by accident; it takes a lot of work. Creating a successful marriage depends on *being* the right partner as much as marrying the right partner. Ask yourself, "What is it like to be married to me?"

Another myth that needs to be dispelled is that some couples are perfect. Have you noticed how much easier it is to solve others' problems and differences than it is to solve your own? We judge others by their actions and ourselves by our intentions—it's easier that way. Perfection is a process, not an event.

The following list was developed by David H. Olsen. If followed, these steps will assist any couple in resolving their differences.

Ten Steps for Resolving Conflicts:
1. Set a time and place for discussion.
2. Define the problem or issue of a disagreement.
3. Talk about how each of you contributes to the problem.
4. List past attempts to resolve the issues that were unsuccessful.
5. Brainstorm ten new ways to resolve the conflict.
6. Discuss and evaluate these possible solutions.
7. Agree on one solution to try.
8. Agree on how each of you will work toward this solution.
9. Set up another meeting to discuss your progress.
10. Reward each other as you each contribute toward this solution.[5]

The following is a compilation of principles and techniques that can be used to resolve differences. This is not a comprehensive list, but just some ideas to help those who need specifics to aid them. Incorporating these techniques may take some effort. Don't expect miracles. Rather, expect a gradual growing awareness of yourself and your thinking processes. As you think this way, also think of how your self-awareness affects your relationship with your spouse and with others. Most alterations that improve yourself and your life will have a positive effect on your relationships with your spouse, family members, and others you associate with.

Key principles when dealing with differences:

- Realize that you can't change your spouse into your ideal person. Accept your differences, and perhaps even appreciate them.
- Compromise is central to marriage.
- Be hard on the problem and soft on the person.
- Keep the focus on one issue at a time, rather than bringing up past issues.
- Don't expect your partner to read your mind.
- If need be, try writing down what's bothering you. This helps clarify your thoughts.
- Nothing is ever accomplished by a raised voice. Make sure your emotional state is under control before you address your spouse. Usually, things that are said in the heat of anger are things you wish you hadn't said when you think about it the next day.
- When you do want to talk to your spouse about an issue, make

sure there are no distractions. Bring up issues at appropriate times and places.

- Don't use absolutes when resolving differences.
- Focus on the effort your partner has made rather than the final outcome of the situation.
- Don't go through your children to communicate with your spouse.
- Don't tell your spouse, "I don't have a problem; you're the one with the problem." If your spouse has a problem, then you have a problem too.
- Don't withdraw by saying you don't want to discuss the issue.
- Focus on the pain your spouse is in, not on the pain they're causing you.
- Don't attack or belittle your spouse.
- The goal of conflict resolution is to try to understand your spouse's view. You might not agree with it, but showing him you are trying to understand his point of view makes it safer to communicate feelings.
- Try not to convey that you have to be right all the time.
- Invite the Spirit of the Lord into your discussion. Be humble, soften your heart, and don't let the discussion escalate.
- Express your positive feelings to your spouse. This might take some effort, but it will help immeasurably to put your differences into perspective.
- From an eternal perspective, the issue at hand is probably not very important at all.
- Most differences are not the issue; they are the battleground or the symptom of the underlying problem.
- The root of most differences is one person not feeling as important or significant as they would like to be, or one person losing control over a given situation.

DIVORCE-PROOFING YOUR MARRIAGE

John Gottman said, "The key to reviving or divorce-proofing a relationship is not in how you handle disagreements, but in how you are with each other when you're not fighting. . . . Strengthen the friendship that is at the heart of any marriage"[6]

Implied in Dr. Gottman's statement is the point that has previously been made. The technique used in resolving differences shouldn't be the main focal point. Rather, look at how you show respect for each other, and decide if you really like to be around each other. Those are the key components that lay the foundation for respect to show through when differences surface.

Some individuals say that a big blowup, one involving all-out yelling and screaming, is good for the relationship. I disagree. To support my conclusion, I refer to an article by Stanley, Howard & Whitton, in which they say, "Overall, how couples argue was more related to divorce potential than was what they argue about."[7]

Why are individuals hesitant to change their thinking and behaviors when it comes to resolving differences? The following are some of the most common fears and hindrances that I have noticed in marriage relationships when couples try to resolve differences include the following:

1. Fear of going outside one's personal comfort zone.
2. The appearance of old habits that are hard to break.
3. Fear of embarrassment, failure, or rejection.
4. Pride.
5. Feeling justified for having angry feelings.
6. Really knowing you're right and the other person is wrong.
7. Not knowing how to resolve differences.
8. Having no desire to resolve differences.
9. Believing that if the world would change, you'd be happier.
10. Believing it's easier to fantasize than it is to face reality.

THE ROLE OF RELIGION

A recently published article showed that religious beliefs are important in helping couples resolve their differences. The study described how religiosity influences marital conflict in 57 highly religious middle-aged couples. The couples reported that religiosity affected the conflict in their marriage at three phases of the conflict process: (1) problem prevention; (2) conflict resolution; and (3) relationship reconciliation. Practitioners may assist religious couples who are struggling with marital conflict by encouraging them to look to religious beliefs and practices.[8]

From this study, we can conclude that religious beliefs and practices will do more to help the couple in the areas of prevention, resolution, and reconciliation than any other technique that could be utilized.

Q: My wife and I have major differences. I was a bad father to our children. I was never there for them but worked hard to make a living. I was not patient with them or my wife. I have recently seen the error of my ways and have made a 180-degree turn. Before, it was my wife encouraging me, but now I am encouraging her to make some alterations so our family can be happier. I am very logical in pointing out to her why we need to resolve our differences. She is having a difficult time seeing the new me. She says I'm just trying to control her to get my way, and she resents that. What can I do?

In answering this question, I will refer to portions of a letter I sent to a husband:

> I do not disagree with any of your logical comments about the importance of the family and what is at stake if the marriage does not work out. However, you are presenting some very logical ideas to her that she interprets as pressure and controlling. I think that she already knows how you feel and the logic of how you see things, and the consequences that will be associated with her decision. May I suggest one additional idea? Talk to her from an emotional or empathetic viewpoint. A genuine, but yet a more feeling oriented approach. Say things like, "I understand that you are confused right now; I know that I've been hard to live with and since I've changed, you probably still have memories of my selfish person from years ago; it must be confusing for you to have memories of how I was such a jerk, yet see the new me; or, it has to be very upsetting to you to feel the way that you do; it must be hard for you to experience the conflict of emotions which I perceive that you might be experiencing. It must be very difficult for you to try and rid yourself of people and programs from controlling you, and then I'm constantly in your face and you perceive me to be controlling you."
>
> I'm not saying that this will work, but I am suggesting that it will take the sting and perceived pressure out of your comments. What it will do is convey to her that you know what she is feeling. It will convey to her that you understand what she is feeling, even though you might not agree with it. There is a difference between understanding how a person feels and agreeing with how the person feels.
>
> The goal in this approach is to present a side of you that she does not see a lot: the ability to be empathetic rather than controlling and pushy. She knows that you do not want to continue in the relationship as it presently is, and neither does she. But try to motivate her with

love, understanding (not agreeing); with softness, yet directness (not controlling), and with consistency rather than logic.

My advice to the husband was that he continue in this approach because it was right, whether she responded positively to it or not. This kind of approach, consistently followed, will make him a better person over time. He is not doing this just to win her over; he is doing it because it's the right thing to do. By viewing his changed behavior in this manner, he will not be wasting his time; rather, he will be investing time into the new him.

Notes

1. Robert C. Dodds, www.wisdomquotes.com/cat_marriage.html.

2. John M. Gottman, *Why Marriages Succeed or Fail* (New York: Simon & Schuster, 1994), 56–58

3. John M. Gottman and Nan Silver, *The Seven Principles for Making Marriage Work* (New York: Three Rivers Press, 1999), 130–33.

4. Gottman and Silver, *The Seven Principles for Making Marriage Work*, 133–40.

5. David H. Olsen, "Ten Steps for Resolving Couple Conflict," www.wartalk.info.

6. Gottman and Silver, *The Seven Principles for Making Marriage Work*, 46.

7. Scott M. Stanley, Howard J. Markman, and Sarah W. Whitton, "Communication, Conflict, and Commitment: Insights on the Foundations of Relationship Success from a National Survey," *Family Process*, 41 (4), 2002, 659–75.

8. N. M. Lambert and D. C. Dollahite, Lambert, "How Religiosity Helps Couples Prevent, Resolve, and Overcome Marital Conflict," *Family Relations: Interdisciplinary Journal of Applied Family Studies*, 55 (4), 2006, 439–49.

Divorce

Q: We used to be so alike, it was almost scary. Eight years later, we are so different. I don't recognize my spouse as the person I married. We lead very separate lives and rarely spend time together. We have tried to do things that used to bring us joy and bring us together, but nothing has worked. Divorce seems so sad, but I see no other alternatives. We practically live as two single people in the same house. Is there anything left we can try?

Q: My parents divorced when I was thirteen years old. Many of my friends' parents have also split up. I've worried for years that I won't know how to have a healthy marriage relationship because I have never really seen a healthy marriage up close. I don't want to go through a divorce of my own because I have already seen the effect it has had on me, my parents, and other family members. Although all these elements are already against me, do I still have a chance at having a happy marriage?

Q: My spouse told me recently that he is involved in an affair and has been for some time. He's not even sure that he wants to continue to try and make our marriage work. While my feelings are mixed, I still feel it's important to forgive him and at least try to move forward in our relationship. I fear what life will be like for our children without their father around, but I am also aware that how I speak about him can greatly influence their view of him. This makes me wonder if divorce would be the best solution.

The following information was obtained from www.divorcerate.org, which is a major resource for providing information on the divorce rates in America and around the world.

Divorce Rates in America

It is frequently reported that the divorce rate in America for first marriages is 50 percent. The Americans for Divorce Reform estimates that "probably, 40 or possibly even 50 percent of marriages will end in divorce if current trends continue."[2]

Some details about the age distribution of divorced persons are shown on the following table.[3]

Age	Women	Men
Under 20	27.6 %	11.7 %
20 to 24	36.6 %	38.8 %
25 to 29	16.4 %	22.3 %
30 to 34	8.5 %	11.6 %
35 to 39	5.1 %	6.5 %

The divorce rate in America for first marriages is 50 percent. The rates for second and third marriages are 67 percent and 74 percent, respectively.[4]

Enrichment Journal provided the following statistics on the divorce rate in America:

- The divorce rate in America for first marriages is 41 percent (because fewer are marrying).
- The divorce rate in America for second marriages is 60 percent.
- The divorce rate in America for third marriages is 73 percent.[5]

Although these statistics vary somewhat, it can be concluded that of those who divorce and then remarry, approximately 66 out of 100 couples will divorce again. Then, if they remarry for the third time, almost 75 out of 100 will divorce. What is the conclusion? Your chances of a successful marriage are better the first time.

BELIEFS ABOUT DIVORCE

I have never met a couple who, on their wedding day, said they wanted a divorce. Yet, I have met couples shortly after that blissful day who indicate that divorce might be the best solution to the negative feelings they are experiencing. Why are they so willing to give up on their relationship so soon after being married?

In *The Good Marriage: How and Why Love Lasts*, Wallerstein and Blakeslee provide insight into the trend of marriages:

> In the past twenty years, marriage in America has undergone a profound, irrevocable transformation, driven by changes in women's roles and the heightened expectations of both men and women. Without realizing it, we have crossed a marital Rubicon. For the first time in our history, the decision to stay married is purely voluntary. Anyone can choose to leave at any time—and everyone knows it, including the children. There used to be only two legal routes out of marriage—adultery and abandonment. Today one partner simply has to say, for whatever reason, "I want out." Divorce is as simple as a trip to the nearest courthouse.
>
> Each year two million adults and a million children in this country are newly affected by divorce. One in two American marriages ends in divorce, and one in three children can expect to experience their parents' divorce. This situation has powerful ripple effects that touch us all. The sense that relationships are unstable affects the family next door, the people down the block, and the other children in the classroom. Feelings of intense anxiety about marriage permeate the consciousness of all young men and women on the threshold of adulthood.[6]

Some believe that divorce is the best and only remedy for a marriage that is in trouble. Once the "D-word" is used, the relationship usually starts to erode. Divorce is held over the head of a spouse as a threat to conform to a set of expectations. In most cases, divorce should never be mentioned or thought of as an appropriate solution. The energy of each spouse needs to be centered on the marriage union and reconciling problem areas. There needs to be less divorce and more regret, sorrow, and change on an individual level.

I cannot play the role of "all-knowing," nor is it my place to tell individuals what to do when it comes to their relationship, because I simply don't know. I can't predict whether a marriage will be successful. I can only do my best to assist a couple in their decision-making process and offer advice, but the future of their relationship has to be up to them. I am responsible to *help* them; I am not responsible *for* them.

WHAT MAKES THE DIFFERENCE?

We all know individuals who are divorced. They are members of our families, neighborhoods, and communities. Every situation is different. Therefore, it is imperative that we do not judge or make a divorcee feel guilty, inferior, or worthless because of his marital status. Couples who get divorced usually have the same problems as those who stay together and work things out. Except for extreme cases of abuse or unremorseful infidelity, I believe that if both partners in a marriage are strongly committed to themselves, to the relationship, and to their children, few divorces would occur.

Divorce can be caused by a spouse feeling he has to have all of his needs met. When those needs are not met, he then believes he is justified in thinking that divorce is the solution. This type of thinking is a reflection of society's philosophy about consumer happiness: "I'm not happy as a customer; therefore, I will return the product for a full refund." This type of thinking is very prevalent, yet highly destructive of a marriage.

In today's culture, it isn't about obligation, duty, or commitment; rather, it is about individual happiness and contentment. If a spouse feels like he has been cheated out of his happiness and isn't getting all that he thought he should get from the marriage, then he feels justified in obtaining a divorce. Where does working constantly at the marriage come into play? Where does the commitment influence the outcome of the marriage relationship?

Some individuals are divorced and happy. Some are divorced and unhappy, and still some couples who are married wish they were divorced. It is not my place to judge those who are divorced, but I would say that in many cases, divorce isn't a cure, nor should it be the first possible solution. I have come to realize that rather than being an escape, divorce often means moving from one bad situation to a worse one.

CAUSES OF DIVORCE

Someone once said that the biggest cause of divorce is marriage. Many say the biggest cause is finances; others say communication. And the list goes on. Whatever the cause may be, divorce is breaking up homes and families. Thinking divorce will cure marital disharmony is, in many cases, a false assumption. Divorce is the consequence of self-centeredness, arrogance, and an unwillingness to change.

The Effects of Marriage on Children

Q: I am not happily married; however, I believe I should stay married because of our children. My wife and I don't argue or fight in front of them, so I don't think they are aware of the coldness and detachment my wife and I are experiencing. Am I just fooling myself, or can we really pull this off?

Simply stated, happy couples make happy parents, and happy parents raise happy children. It is logical to assume that the parents' relationship has an effect, either positive or negative, on their children. More research needs to be done in this area. However, I will emphasize some major points of an article by Dr. Sharma, who writes concerning the effect parents have on children:

> We all know that unhappy married couples exhibit emotional withdrawal, conflict, and acrimony. However, what may not be so obvious is that their interaction with babies also changes as a result of their relationship with each other. Gottman observed that when these unhappy couples played with their children, the children didn't smile as much as children with happily married parents. These couples were not in sync and often excluded each other.
>
> The effect of their disharmony on the babies was even more striking. The babies showed accelerated heart rate even when the parents were not arguing or fighting. How the tension between the parents is communicated to a tiny infant at a physical level is not yet understood.
>
> Some parents think that because they don't fight in front of their children or send them to their rooms as soon as they start fighting, their conflict does not have an impact on their children. This provides a false assurance. Children absorb parental tension as surely as they breathe the air around them.
>
> Children from troubled marriages have a higher incidence of aggressive behaviors, truancy, peer conflicts, depression, and lower academic achievement. That's the bad news. The good news is that the children of happily married couples possess better social skills, have lower incidence of aggressive behaviors and depression, possess better social skills, and receive better grades.[7]

The article goes on to say that the greatest gift parents can give their children is their relationship with each other. The strongest protection that you can offer your children is time and attention, and a strong emotional connection and involvement.[8]

Effects of Children on Divorce

According to the Discovery Channel, couples with children have a slightly lower rate of divorce than childless couples.

Sociologists believe that childlessness is also a common cause of divorce. The absence of children leads to loneliness and weariness, and even in the United States, at least 66 percent of all divorced couples are childless.[9]

Effects of Divorce on Children

Divorce has far-reaching effects. It's hard on the two main individuals involved, their families, and especially their children. It is difficult to generalize how all children are affected by divorce, since each case is unique. However, from the following research, some insightful conclusions were reached that couples should be aware of before they start divorce proceedings:

"Parental divorce approximately doubled the odds that offspring would see their own marriages end in divorce. Offspring with maritally distressed parents who remained continuously married did not have an elevated risk of divorce. . . . Offspring with divorced parents have an elevated risk of seeing their own marriages end in divorce because they hold a comparatively weak commitment to the norm of lifelong marriage."[10]

Other studies could be discussed, but most, if not all, would come to the same conclusion: in most situations, divorce has a negative effect on the children.

When Is Divorce Justified?

I mentioned previously that in many cases, I am a poor judge of when divorce is justified. Over the years I have learned that the power to either dissolve or make a marriage work lies solely within the two individuals involved in the relationship. Others can counsel, give advice, or even tell them what to do, but ultimately the decision falls on the married couple.

One couple, when asked how they stayed married for over thirty years, responded, "Because neither one of us decided to quit on the same day."

In some cases, divorce seems like the obvious solution. These cases might involve abuse, incest, or infidelity. The abuse would not necessarily have to be physical; it could be verbal or emotional. If repeated attempts to reconcile the marriage have been made, and yet someone's dignity and integrity as a human being is still being degraded to the point where he has little self-esteem left, there might be sufficient justification for divorce. Even though these types of situations occur, more often I see couples who say they divorced because of personality differences, lack of communication, or falling out of love. In my opinion, these reasons do not justify breaking marital vows.

In some situations, divorce is the only reasonable decision. This could include circumstances in which the husband abuses his wife or children, is a drug addict and is constantly stealing money for his addiction, doesn't financially provide for his family, or is constantly unfaithful to his wife and children. These extreme situations could justify divorce in order to remove the wife and children from the situation so they can move ahead with their lives.

Notes

1. www.divorcerate.org.

2. Ibid.

3. Ibid.

4. Jennifer Baker, www.divorcerate.org.

5. www.divorcerate.org

6. J. S. Wallerstien and S. Blakesleeb, *The Good Marriage: How and Why Love Lasts* (Boston: Houghton Mifflin, 1995), 6–7.

7. Vijai P. Sharma, "Happy Marriages, Happy Children," 16 Jan. 2004, http://www.mindpub.com/art422.htm.

8. Ibid.

9. www.divorcerate.org

10. P. R. Amato and D. D. DeBoer, "The Transmission of Marital Instability Across Generations: Relationship Skills or Commitment to Marriage?" *Journal of Marriage and Family*, 63(4), Oct. 2001, 1038–51.

Effort

Q: I have been married for twenty-five years, and my husband says he loves being married but does not see the need to put forth more effort. There are no major problems, but I feel sort of stuck in the same place. The love has not diminished, nor has the arguing increased, but to him, everything is established and great the way it is. On the other hand, I think our marriage is in a rut, and I want our relationship to continue to grow. What can I do with my unwilling husband?

Q: My husband and I have been married for twenty years. We have a good marriage, but I know it could be better. Some areas of our relationship have become stagnant and we just tolerate it, thinking that it could be worse. We would both like to improve our good marriage and make it a better marriage. What are the ingredients for a successful marriage?

Have you lost that feeling of loving and being loved? Is everything just work, paying the bills, mopping the floor, mowing the lawn, and taking care of the family? Have you stopped saying, "I love you," daily?

In a recent seventeen-year study, researchers noted:

> The big secret to a happy long-term relationship is no big secret at all. What it takes to improve a marriage is generally common sense. But the research in this field indicates that, once again, common sense is not always so common. It is obvious that only 10–15 percent of couples are able to keep doing most of the things that seemed to come so easily when they first fell in love. For reasons that researchers don't completely understand, this small proportion of couples pay attention

to these essentials and keep doing the things which result in fulfilling relationships. Those individuals in a marriage relationship are exceptional in no other way that they can tell. They are not smarter, richer, better looking, "sexier," or more educated than you. This is encouraging. It says that anyone who is knowledgeable and attentive can have a happy, intimate relationship.[1]

People often believe that marriage is successful only if the right two people come together. That assumption is false. Marriages don't succeed automatically. Couples who build happy, safe, and successful marriages pay the price to do so. It takes constant effort; it doesn't happen by chance.

Wallerstein and Blakeslee conducted a study to find out what people mean when they say their marriages are "happy." To what did they attribute their happiness? Were they happy from the start, and if not, what made the difference? Quoting from the book, Wallerstein summarizes some of her conclusions with the following statements:

> I began each interview by asking, "Tell me what's good about this marriage." My second question was, "What's disappointing about your marriage? . . ."
>
> [The couples] made it clear that they were not happy all the time. Many admitted that at times they wanted out. Some confessed that on occasion they felt they had made a mistake. But each person felt strongly that on balance in their marriage, there was a goodness of fit in needs, wishes, and expectations. Although everyone was reluctant to define love, they spoke movingly, often lyrically, about how much they valued, respected, and enjoyed the other person and how appreciative they were of the other's responsiveness to their needs. . . ."
>
> Others emphasized the security that marriage afforded. . . ."
>
> Happy marriages are not carefree. There are good times and bad times, and certainly partners may face serious crises together or separately. Happily married husbands and wives get depressed, fight, lose jobs, struggle with the demands of the workplace and the crises of infants and teenagers, and confront sexual problems. They cry and yell and get frustrated. They come from sad, abusive, neglectful backgrounds as well as from more stable families. . . ."
>
> If [a couple] can appreciate the myriad ways that people grow and change through the years and realize that a happy, lasting marriage is challenged and rebuilt every day, then they will have acquired the only map there is for a successful lifetime journey together.[2]

Marriage means work, and must be worked on daily. It should not be viewed as a chore, but rather as an opportunity to convey your love to your spouse. Among couples I have seen, a significant attribute that creates satisfaction in a marriage is expressing affection on a regular basis. Couples who indulge in frequent terms of endearment, nonsexual touching such as hugs and hand-holding, and tokens of affection such as small gifts feel fulfilled in their marriage.

Many couples allow expressions of affection to dwindle because they associate them with only being essential at the beginning of a relationship. They think candy, flowers, cards, and having fun together is just a prelude to a real relationship. On the contrary, the little things keep energy in your association and are vital to maintain your relationship.

Marriage takes time. Mother Teresa, leader of the Missionaries of Charity, stated, "Today we have no time. The father and the mother are so busy . . . I always say: Family first. If you are not there, how will your love grow for one another?"[3]

Notes

1. A. Stutzer and Frey, "Does Marriage Make People Happy, or Do Happy People Get Married?" *Journal of Socio-Economics*, 35 [2], 2006 326–47.

2. Judith S. Wallerstein and Sandra Blakeslee, *The Good Marriage: How and Why Love Lasts* (Boston: Houghton Mifflin, 1995), 11–15.

3. Jaya Chaliha and Edward le Joly, comp., *The Joy in Loving: A Guide to Daily Living with Mother Teresa* (New York: Viking, 1996), 146.

Empty Nesters

Q: Now that all of our children have left home, my wife and I are spending more time together. Sometimes I wonder if I really even know her. What are some ways to overcome this strangeness and get to know one another again?

There has been a steady increase in the number of divorces among couples who have been married thirty or more years. Many long-term married couples get divorced after the kids leave home. They realize too late that their children kept them together. Other couples divorce during the empty nest years because they can't handle the health issues and the sense of an uncertain future, and they feel overwhelmed by spending too much time together.

The good news is that with positive communication and preparation for this phase of your marriage, the empty nest years can be tremendously enjoyable and full of new beginnings. Now that the kids have left home, what comes next?

Empty nesters can focus on certain areas to help ease the transition into this phase of life. Look over the following lists and discover which issues apply to your particular situation.

Things you will notice right away:

- You may feel a sense of emptiness and loneliness.
- You are delighted to see emails from your kids or have them call you.
- Your grocery bills are lower.

- Abandoned pets need to be fed.
- There is food in the refrigerator.
- The house stays clean.
- You look forward to receiving pictures from the kids.
- You only have to wash clothes and towels once a week.
- Your home is quiet.
- There is hot water when you want it.
- The phone rings less.
- Your water bill takes a dive.
- You can use the computer whenever you want.
- Your attic is full of boxes of the kids' mementos and belongings they need stored for awhile.
- You may keep some of your kids' favorite stuffed animals or toys where you can see them.

Things you need to discuss:

- Your hopes and dreams for the future.
- Expectations.
- The sense of grief you are both feeling in dealing with the kids leaving home.
- Financial concerns.
- Health issues, including menopause.
- Downsizing.
- Changing roles.
- Where you want to live for the rest of your life.
- Boomerang kids.
- Grandchildren.
- Aging parents.
- Getting in one another's way and on one another's nerves.
- The importance of being versus doing.
- Travel.
- Having fun together.

Things you need to do:

- Seek counseling if your empty nest marriage is showing signs of withdrawal, alienation, and negativity.
- Accept the grief you feel and know that both men and women experience it. Empty nest dads may feel a sense of regret over things

they didn't do and time they didn't spend with their children.

- Limit how often you call your kids.
- Don't place guilt trips on your kids, especially during the holidays.
- Keep lists of each kid's favorite foods for his visits or care packages.
- Develop a flexible mind-set and be open to change.
- Work on becoming friends with your adult children.
- Don't rush into volunteer roles, travel, taking classes, moving, or emptying out a child's room. You have plenty of time.
- Schedule dates with each other.
- Make a list of things you have never done but would like to do.
- Make some short-term and long-term plans on how you will spend your money and time.
- If you are thinking about downsizing, see if you can de-clutter and simplify your life without moving.
- Before moving to a new location, make sure you have truly double-checked your tax situation and benefits from selling and buying, and analyzed maintenance and utility costs in the new location.
- Don't make assumptions about what your spouse is thinking or wanting to do.[1]

Marital burnout doesn't happen to empty nest couples who continue to be sensitive to and aware of one another. You can turn the second half of your marital journey into a delightful time of discovery and joy.

There are many reasons for marital burnout, but many of these couples divorce because they focused so much of their lives on their children and not on each other. Couples find themselves fearful of aging, depressed over their situation, and unsure about their future. This situation can be rectified by getting away, just the two of you. You should plan a weekly date, an occasional overnight stay, and dates with other couples in your situation so you can discuss your concerns about the future. Do this while the children are at home so that when they leave, the shock of becoming reacquainted with your spouse isn't so dramatic.

Couples need to be more aware of one another's feelings and thoughts. This should always be done while the children are still at home, and even more so when they leave. When the children do leave, a couple feels as if they have completed their life's purpose and won't be contributing anymore to their family or society. On the contrary, when the children do leave home, couples should remember that parenting never stops and the couple needs to regroup, refocus, and refresh their marriage. They need to find purpose in being together and learn to accept their new roles of empty nesters, grandparents, and retirees. If they don't, their relationship will be meaningless, and they will most likely join the empty nesters whose marriages fall apart.

Notes

1. David H. Arp Jr., Claudia S. Arp, Scott M. Stanley, et. al., *Empty Nesting: Reinventing Your Relationship When the Kids Leave Home* (Hoboken: John Wiley and Sons, 2000), 10–11, 13, 47.

Expectations

Q: My spouse and I have been married for eight months. Being married is fun, but it's harder than either of us expected. I want to be all that I can be for my husband, and he works hard for me, but sometimes we just don't live up to the expectations we have for one another. Sometimes it feels like we're just "playing house," but I want us to feel like we have a "real" relationship, not just one where we are trying to fulfill these ambiguous expectations and roles. What advice do you have for us to either fulfill one another's expectations, or to help us develop realistic expectations?

Q: Sheila and Paul have been married for three years. Sheila feels like she is trying to do all she can to improve their marriage, but she sometimes wonders if she is just going through the motions, because nothing she does seems to improve the situation. Sheila and Paul have not been arguing and fighting much lately, but they don't seem to be as close as they once were. Sheila is not even sure what Paul expects of their marriage anymore, or what part she is to play.

SHARE EXPECTATIONS

Make sure your expectations are realistic and attainable. Sharing them with your spouse is critical if you want a successful marriage. When you don't share your expectations, disillusionment will most likely become an everyday experience. Many, if not most, expectations of marriage are based on idealized myths that have been developed over the years by watching movies or reading books that portray marriage in an idealistic way. When realities within a relationship do not match the myth, one or both partners may think they've made a terrible mistake and want to remove themselves from the relationship. Or they may try to change their "flawed" partner into the "ideal" partner.

Facing Dissimilar Expectations

Now that the honeymoon is over and reality has set in, some adjustments are necessary. Let's face it: We each come to the marriage with thinking (usually not outwardly stated), "My past was okay. Just look at me, I turned out fine." It's hard to give up our currently held opinions. If your partner holds a different notion on a specific topic, then you might think your job is to convert your spouse to your way of thinking. Wrong! Although tempting, tempers may flare and nothing will be accomplished. After all, who wants to be forced to give up a way of thinking that has produced a great family (of the past) and an emotionally mature individual (currently standing before a spouse he perceives as imperfect)? What is the solution?

When your spouse does not meet your expectations willingly, your voice and energy levels rise until you say, "If you really loved me, you would have my dinner ready on time." If that statement does not produce the desired results, a threatening tone will then follow: "I'll get even with you because of that."

The spouse who resorts to demands and threats will usually not get the desired results. Reminding your spouse of your wants and needs in a loving and caring way will usually produce the desired behavior. But if you are demanding, disrespectful, and angry, you will usually produce resentment within your spouse, and he or she will resist.

Our perception of events becomes our reality. With two people clinging onto a different set of reality, who would want to voluntarily give up their ideas? Naturally, we would want to convince others of the importance and significance of our beliefs and practices. Research has shown that cognitions, particularly exaggerated, or rigidly held personal rules of living account for almost all marital conflict. As we change dysfunctional expectations into more flexible compromises, we'll find that we have more positive feelings for our spouse.

Of course, we need to hold on to our core beliefs and values. But most of our rigidly held beliefs are a result of pride and stubbornness.

Prioritize beliefs, attitudes, and opinions. If they are not core, modify them to become more like what your spouse desires. Why not? As you look deep into yourself, don't be so narrow in your thinking. Work with your spouse to achieve worthwhile expectations and goals.

ORIGIN OF EXPECTATIONS

Prior to marriage, all couples have expectations of how marriage should be. These expectations are based on past experiences and modeling of parents or significant others.

Some couples go into marriage with unrealistic expectations and are upset when their spouse does not meet them. The following lists will help you determine if you married for the right reasons and if you have realistic expectations in your marriage relationship.

Did you:
- Marry someone you love and respect?
- Marry someone with similar values?
- Marry someone who wants to help you be the best person you can be?
- Marry someone whose goals you support?
- Talk about important issues that come up in all marriages (such as parenting), before marriage?

Or did you:
- Marry because it seemed like the thing to do?
- Expect your spouse to change after marriage?
- Think marriage would solve all your problems?
- Expect marriage to be one long honeymoon?
- Marry because you felt uncomfortable about premarital intimacy?

After answering these questions, a person needs to ask himself, "Why do I believe the way I do? How were my opinions formed? Why do I hold strongly to some opinions and not to others? How are my opinions linked to my expectations? Is it possible to let go of or alter my opinions? If so, which ones am I willing to let go of or change?"

DETERMINING YOUR EXPECTATIONS

Do you really know what your spouse wants in life? Knowing the answer to this question is a major key to a successful relationship. It is unrealistic to expect your spouse to intuitively know your expectations. It is easy to impose or project your own wishes or ideas of what you like onto your spouse, but that's missing the point. If you really want to make your partner happy, take the time to discover the little things that will make him happy, and then give these things to them. This will make him feel loved and appreciated by letting him know you are sensitive to and truly understand what he desires.

The following exercise is provided to assist you in determining your expectations, and which ones need to be altered. I have couples complete the following exercise which I have developed. This exercise can be done prior to marriage or at any time during.

- On an 8½ x 11 lined piece of paper, on your computer, or in a journal, list 28 expectations you have of yourself, your spouse, and the relationship (I will be the major money earner; my spouse will pay the bills; we will date regularly; and so forth).
- Put an "NN" by those expectations that are non-negotiable (only mark 2–3 expectations). This implies that your mind is absolutely made up and will not change on these particular issues.
- Prioritize the remaining expectations by putting the number 1 by those that are the most important (no more than five); the number 2 by those that are second in importance (no more than five); the number 3 by those that are third in importance; and proceed through numbers 4 and 5, indicating approximately five expectations for each number. Those with the number 5 by them are the least important in comparison to the others, but they are still important.
- Now share the list with your spouse and read his list as well; you will quickly find discrepancies between your lists.
- Discuss why number 1 on your partner's list is not even mentioned on your sheet. Perhaps it is implied in another category, or was inadvertently left off. Whatever the reason, the discrepancy provides an opportunity for discussion and adjustment. Attention should be given to discrepancies listed under the numbers 1 and 5, since they are more polarized. Don't spend as much time on numbers 3 and 4 since they are closer together.

You may have to recalibrate some of your expectations in your relationship. You and your spouse will have to compromise. This exercise will help you see and hear what is important to both of you. You will see that each of you will win some things and lose others, but each of you will have a say in the necessary modifications.

ADJUSTING EXPECTATIONS

Couples in satisfying marriages have had to adjust some of their expectations. They have been honest with themselves about what they need from, and what they are willing to give to, the relationship. Most important, they make an effort to regularly communicate their feelings and needs to each other.

When couples are struggling with expectations for the marriage, I will have both individuals rate their perception of the marriage relationship in the following ten areas. These areas are those that I believe are important to achieving a successful marriage. Each individual is to rate the marriage on a scale of 1 to 10, 1 being low concurrence and 10 being in total concurrence.

1. Common goals and values
2. Commitment to marital growth
3. Communication skills
4. Affection and appreciation
5. Creating use of conflict
6. Agreement on male and female roles
7. Cooperation and teamwork
8. Sexual fulfillment
9. Money management
10. Parenting cooperation (or general decision-making if there are no children yet)

After each partner has individually rated the relationship, compare your scores. The goal of the above assignment is not to be exactly alike in all areas, but to use this as a vehicle to discuss expectations in the marriage relationship and make any necessary adjustments.

Marriage is not a substitute for a good self-image, a happy childhood, or a fulfilling job. All marriages go through adjustments where the reality of sharing yourself, dreams, and expectations with someone else becomes a major task. For some, this is very difficult. For others, the task is not so complex. A willingness to focus on *what* is right for the relationship, rather than on *who* is right, will go a long way in achieving a more solid marriage relationship.

Expectations change over the years, necessitating constant communication and honesty with each other. Acknowledge the effort your spouse makes to meet your needs and expectations.

Every person has a need to be loved, appreciated, valued, and accepted. When one spouse is trying to meet the other's expectations, it is important to positively reward the efforts, even though the performance may not be perfect. A wife might tell her husband, "I appreciate the effort you've made in helping me clean the windows," rather than, "Is that the best you can do? I'd better just do it myself." When you acknowledge and reward the effort, your spouse is more likely to try again. When both the effort and the outcome are on target, a sincere "Thank you, that means a lot to me," will be the most valuable motivator in altering behaviors.

COMPARING OUR RELATIONSHIP TO OTHERS

When we compare ourselves to others, we always come up short. That's because we're comparing our marriage's weaknesses with another couple's strong points. The couples I know do not have perfect marriages. They have very good ones, but not perfect ones. They see marriage as a journey, not a destination that you arrive at and then stop progressing. We all need to make adjustments to make our relationship work.

Finances

Q: I've heard that money problems are a leading factor in the breakup of many marriages. I have two questions for you: (1) What are the common financial pitfalls that couples run into? (2) What counsel can you give us to help avoid those pitfalls?

Before answering these questions, a few points need to be made. There are organizations and books that go into great detail concerning better money management; however, that is not my purpose in answering these questions. Instead, I want to show how finances play a significant role in the marriage relationship. No matter what the trends or studies conclude, every marriage has its own unique DNA, financial and otherwise. Most marriages don't fit neatly into the classic stereotypes.

A study published in *Smart Money Magazine* in February 2004 surveyed 1,016 married or cohabiting adults on money and marriage. In the study, more than 70 percent of those surveyed said they talked to their partner about money at least once a week; however, not all of that talk was truthful. Roughly 40 percent of both men and women admitted lying about the cost of something they bought.[1] The survey also discovered that control "is the quiet culprit lurking behind many, if not most, marriage and money issues."[2]

"When a couple has any problem, it's because of a power imbalance," says Donna Laikind, a marriage and family therapist who counsels couples on money issues in New York and Connecticut. "Money is not seen as the commodity that it should be," she says. "It's fraught with layers and layers of meaning."[3]

In his article entitled "The Credit Trap," in the August 2001 edition of *Marriage & Families*, Bernard Poduska provides some ways to avoid debt:

1. Pay cash for as many things as possible.
2. Reduce your living expenses.
3. Stop going into debt.
4. Get out of debt.[4]

Some people are so deep in the credit trap that the steps described above, while helpful, will not set them free. Here are some signs that you are in serious trouble:

1. Spending to or beyond your credit limits.
2. Saving no money for emergencies.
3. Not knowing exactly how much you owe.
4. Making late payments or missing payments.
5. Applying for additional credit cards.
6. Consolidating loans.
7. Using more than 20 percent of your take-home pay to pay debts.
8. Deceiving your spouse about the amount spent or owed.
9. Debts being turned over to collection agencies.[5]

There is much information and help on finances available through books and the Internet. If a couple discovers that each month they are getting further in debt, that is reason enough to sit down together and discuss their finances. It may even be necessary to seek outside help. Couples sometimes use money as their battleground to show control and resentment toward each other. This is not to say that all financial problems are behavioral problems. Most often, financial issues come when the couple continually goes into debt for unnecessary things. Last, not notifying your spouse of such behavior is much more than simply a financial issue, and needs to be addressed as such.

Notes

1. Jena McGregor, "Love & Money," *Smart Money Magazine*, 9 Feb. 2004.
2. Ibid.
3. Donna Laikind, as quoted by Jena McGregor, "Love and Money."

4. Bernard Poduska, "The Credit Trap." *Marriage & Families*, Aug. 2001, www.marriageandfamilies.byu.edu

5. Ibid.

forgiveness

Q: I love my wife, and I think I always will love her. However, I recently learned that she's been unfaithful to me. I am so hurt, so angry, and so confused. She has apologized numerous times and we have both committed to make our marriage work again, but I have so many feelings of disappointment and betrayal that seem to stop me from moving forward. I have a hard time fully letting go of my grudge. What are some ways I can overcome the feelings of resentment, anger, betrayal, and hurt I feel toward my wife?

Q: My husband is an incredible person—that's why I married him. Lately, however, there are little things he does that drive me crazy. I know they're insignificant things I ought to be able to ignore, but I have a hard time doing just that. What can I do to forgive him and remember the important reasons I had for marrying him?

Q: My wife, Susan, and I have been having somewhat of a rocky time getting along. She seems to continually hold grudges against me for things I've said and done in the past. Because of the constant grudges she has against me, I've also been more angry than usual in all areas of my life. What can we do to implement the principle of forgiveness in our marriage?

The more ordinary hurts and disappointments in a marriage may not cut so deeply, but they tend to accumulate and to fester if we can't find some way to come to terms with them. They include a multitude of common sins (squeezing the toothpaste tube in the middle, everyday miscommunications, inattention, and the like). Each is small enough in itself, but if we take even these small problems personally, or if we see them as evidence of our partner's lack of consideration, they will drive an enormous wedge between us and our spouse. It is essential for us to forgive each other for such momentary lapses, and even for characteristic flaws. . . . For most of us, [our partner's basic] goodness more than compensates for our partner's human fallibility. When we allow ourselves to see our partner's strengths—courage, commitment, fidelity, friendship, and so on—it is usually clear that the goodness outweighs the foibles. Our ability to see the big picture can go a long way toward encouraging us to practice generosity as we confront each other's imperfections. . . . It is far easier to forgive a hurtful action if you believe that it was inadvertent. There is usually room for this belief because we can never know the reasons for someone's actions with certainty. . . . Given this uncertainty, it seems wise to give your partner the benefit of the doubt whenever possible. When you feel hurt, look carefully to see if the offense was the result of an honest mistake or a weakness. For most of us, most of the time, our partner's misdeeds are mistakes or a result of imperfections. It can be difficult to see something that hurt us as an error, because when we feel hurt or disappointed it is easier to see our spouse's action or inaction as intentional or mean-spirited.[1]

I firmly believe that forgiveness is one of the greatest qualities we can develop. Dr. Bernard Poduska has suggested ten areas in which we could ask for forgiveness from our spouse. Forgive me for:

1. Not always being your friend.
2. Not placing you as my number-one priority in life.
3. Not showing my appreciation.
4. Not being there when you needed me.
5. Not accepting a less than perfect you.
6. The times I have been selfish.
7. The promises implied, or explicit, that I have broken.
8. Neglecting your hopes or dreams.
9. Not helping you reach a greater level of spirituality.
10. Not forgiving you.[2]

Having a strong commitment to the marriage relationship fosters forgiveness. When offended by your spouse, set aside some time to mourn, grieve, and recover from the shock of the betrayal. But the substantial difference between the victim who forgives and the one who holds a grudge is eventually moving past these feelings. The victim is entitled to feel anger, shock, loss, hurt, and other similar feelings, but he must move on. He must redirect his energies because of the commitment he has to the relationship.

In order to truly forgive, you must look at the big picture. Looking at the positives of the relationship is essential. Since none of us do marriage perfectly, an "attitude of latitude" needs to be developed. This does not mean we tolerate persistent behaviors that distract from the marriage or the dignity of another person, but it does mean that we do not judge. We merely forgive. It is easy to judge others by their actions and judge ourselves by our intentions. With these necessary ingredients actively present in the relationship, miracles will take place. The greatest miracle I have seen is the healing of a broken relationship. In order for miracles to take place, humility and forgiveness need to exist in the marriage.

Notes

1. Blaine J. Fowers, *Beyond the Myth of Marital Happiness* (San Francisco: Jossey-Bass Publishers, 2000), 183.

2. Bernard Poduska, "Forgiveness, parts i–x," series of articles under *Save Your Marriage*, marriage.lifetips.com.

Friendship

Q: Friendship doesn't seem like a trait the world emphasizes when talking about love. But friendship is very important, especially if a couple wants to make their relationship last. How can my wife and I improve the friendship aspect of our marriage?

Friendship needs to be cultivated. If, at the beginning of your marriage, you don't have many things in common, cultivate them through the years. I once worked with a couple who reported that they didn't even like visiting the same places; so they took separate vacations. While he went on his vacation, she would stay home and take care of the children. I'm not talking about a day at the mall, or an overnight stay in a neighboring town. I'm talking about Mexico, France, or some other exotic location. The message they were giving to each other was that they could have a better time in these places without their spouse. The couple eventually got a divorce.

You don't have to do everything together, but you do need to spend time seeing or doing things together in order to develop commonalities. As an example, going to a fabric store will never be on the top of my list of fun places to go. My wife, however, could spend hours in such a place. Many times she'll go by herself, but there are times when we are out shopping together and she needs to stop by the fabric store for just a minute and I'll go with her. I don't try to play the martyr; I go because *we* need the experience.

You and your spouse need to make opportunities to do things together—don't wait for them to magically happen. Go camping and shopping together, coach your child's sports team, and bring the rest of the family to the games to cheer.

Look for things you're both interested in, such as photography, bird-watching, scrapbooking, and any other activity you can think of. Involving each other in joint activities, not parallel activities, contributes to the well-being, friendship, and vitality of the marriage. The underlying message is that you enjoy being together and you are building your friendship in anything you do.

A married couple should enjoy spending time together. Ideally, they would want to be with each other more than anyone else. I'm aware of husbands who work late so they don't have to spend more time with their wife. Can you imagine? When married couples are friends, they spend time together. Small moments of silence are not uncomfortable; both small talk and discussions about in-depth issues are acceptable. It really comes down to both of you being comfortable being together, no matter what you are doing.

Many couples I work with who have been married for many years indicate that it isn't the romance that keeps them together, but rather the deep, caring friendship they share, and the ability to enjoy each other's company. These couples also have similar interests and values. Most important, though, they are *friends*.

Honesty

Q: I have been married for ten years, and during that time my spouse has constantly lied to me. He now tells me he's ready to start over and promises he'll never lie to me again. Of course, I've heard this dozens of times. What can we each do so we can trust again? Can it ever be like it was before all this dishonesty?

Honesty is one of the basic requirements in a healthy marriage, and it is vital that you be open and truthful with your spouse. The principle of honesty goes as far back as the Bible, where we are commanded not to lie or steal. Even though prisons are full of people who have broken the law by being dishonest in some aspect, they represent the minority of people. Honesty is a value adhered to by the majority of the population.

A strong marriage relationship is grounded on honesty and trust. Because the marriage relationship is so emotionally close, any tendencies to be dishonest can ruin the best of relationships. Without honesty, problems that may destroy the relationship can stay hidden for years. Honesty is the only way you and your spouse will ever come to understand each other. After all, if you can't be honest with the person you share your life with, who can you be honest with? You should do everything you can to avoid giving your spouse any reason to believe that you are dishonest with him.

Many forms of dishonesty stem from the desire to get something for nothing, or to hide a negative behavior from others. Is there a difference between truthfulness and honesty? According to the dictionary, truth is called honesty, and honesty, truth. But in reality, there probably is a difference. Truth is more of an objective issue. Truthfulness deals with facts. Did something happen, or didn't it? Is what you said accurate? Honesty deals more with emotions, sense of self, and integrity. A person can just tell the truth (say what he has to say to be safe), or a person can be honest.

Can honesty create problems in marriage? Sometimes couples are truthful about the facts but not honest about how they feel. If asked a question, they may answer truthfully, but unless asked, they will not acknowledge certain events or feelings. Is that being honest? Even if they do answer, it often isn't honest. You are being dishonest when someone asks you what's bothering you and you tell them nothing, even though you really do have something on your mind.

Now, in specific reference to the question asked on the previous page, there are three main questions being asked.

1. **What can we each do so we can trust again?** I suggest that couples use "measured honesty," so they share important feelings in an atmosphere of love and support, using self-discipline and sincerity rather than hostility.

   Sometimes individuals cannot be honest with their negative feelings because they have a hard time recognizing and accepting them and don't know what to do about them. Other times, they don't share pessimistic feelings because they've learned that when they do, the conversation ends in a heated argument. Some have never learned how to share feelings appropriately with anyone. If you are not honest about your feelings, those emotions build up and will later be expressed as anger, jealousy, or rage. Unless you tell your spouse what you are feeling, he will end up guessing when he sees negative behavior. Couples need to realize the strength that comes from sharing negative feelings with each other.

2. **Can it ever be like it was before all the dishonesty?** Most likely, no—at least not within a short period of time. The husband has lost his right to be trusted because of his past statements and behavior. Trust can be built again, but he will have to earn that trust day by day. Ultimately, trust can be restored to the marriage, but it will take time. Can the marriage be just as loving as before? Yes. It even has the potential to be more loving than before all the dishonesty took place. To truly have things go back to the way they were, the couple must engage in sensitive dialogue and begin

to process what has happened. Then the healing and forgiveness can begin.

3. **How can I work on completely forgiving?** For more in-depth information, go to the chapter entitled "Forgiveness." However, a short summary here will emphasize key factors in the healing process.

Healing is a process, not an immediate event. But over a period of time, the initial reason for the pain can change in its appearance. This change occurs because our perception of the dishonesty has changed. Often, several positive experiences can begin to replace the pain. We cannot change what has already taken place, so changing what we can change—such as altering our perception and understanding, and remembering positive experiences—can replace the hurt caused by the dishonest actions.

The ultimate forgiveness occurs when the intense negative feelings that we once had no longer exist. We might remember events, but the wrenching of those events upon us is not present. The only way to ultimately rid one of the emotions of dishonest acts imposed upon us is through having our hearts softened so we can forgive those who have taken advantage of us over the years.

STEPS FOR HEALING

The following steps are necessary parts of the healing process that a couple must go through after dishonesty has disrupted their relationship.

1. Accept it has happened.
2. Mourn—this is necessary.
3. Express hurt feelings appropriately.
4. Understand why the behavior occurred.
5. See how sincere your spouse is to not repeat his mistakes.
6. Put yourself in your spouse's shoes.
7. Realize that the healing will be a slow process.
8. Know that there will be doubts.
9. Start to trust your spouse again on the little things.
10. Make a list of the good qualities your spouse possesses, to remind both of you of the positive traits he has.
11. Use religious means for comfort.

Humility

Q: I have a tendency to believe I am right most of the time, and I often hold grudges. I'm not married yet, but I already fear that these characteristics will negatively impact my marriage. What can I do to change?

In order to forgive, one must first be humble. John Beebe says:

> Humility, loyalty, and devotion . . . are required to achieve mutual understanding in any marriage. . . . Therefore, humility is needed to build not just understanding, but mutual understanding in a relationship. Mutual understanding implies more than just understanding in general. Mutual means a common, shared, joint, or reciprocal state, in which the understanding goes both ways. Each spouse has understanding for the other and of "them" as an entity. This sort of understanding fosters respect, appreciation, and deeper love. In a sense, then, humility becomes an important contributor to respect developing in a marriage. And without respect, it becomes very difficult for any marriage to be satisfying, or to last.[1]

Besides being a religious word with spiritual connotations, the importance of *humility* in a marriage relationship has also been written about in scientific literature. Most individuals would agree that understanding, respect, and appreciation are essential ingredients for a successful marriage. But further exploration into how these qualities are established is not explored. Humility is necessary. Everyone must ask himself, "How do I acquire humility?" If you focus on pleasing your spouse more than yourself, you will quarrel less. All it takes for a positive change to occur is for you or your spouse to be humble and respond differently to the issues and situations that come up.

Notes

1. John Beebe, response to Anita von Raffay's paper, "Why It Is Difficult to See the Animal as a Helpful Object," *Journal of Analytical Psychology*, Vol. 45 (4), Oct. 2000, 565–68.

Humor

Q: My wife and I used to laugh together all the time. We have been in some tough circumstances, and the trials we have faced seem to have taken away some of the energy and excitement we had for life. We realize that we don't laugh together as often as we used to. How important is humor in a marriage? What are some things we can do to bring more humor into our lives?

Q: My wife often says "just kidding" when I am the brunt of her jokes. It doesn't matter if it's just at home or out with our friends. Most of the time I believe her and feel she is not intentionally trying to hurt my feelings. However, I sometimes get a sense that she is deliberate in her comments and wants to punish or criticize me. I'm afraid that if I tell her my concerns, she will say what she has before—that I am too sensitive and need to learn to take a joke. What can I do to make her take me seriously and see how her comments really affect me?

WHAT IS HUMOR?

Humor is the quality of seeing the ridiculousness or silliness in a situation. Good humor is appealing and fun-loving, and can diffuse anger or frustration. Using humor inappropriately can lead to mocking or making fun.

Humor is necessary to lighten stress and to bring a bit of leaven to the relationship. Everyone has some degree of humor or a bright side that can be used or relied on more in the relationship.

A research project examined the importance of humor appreciation in marital adjustment in two groups of spouses, one with marital problems (97 men and 96 women) and the other representing the general population (26 men and 47 women). There was less humor appreciation in the distressed sample group, and appreciation of a spouse's humor correlated significantly with the general state of the marriage. Failure to appreciate the spouse's sense of humor seemed to be a significant indicator of marital distress.[1]

SEEING THE HUMOROUS SIDE

It is possible for individuals to learn to lighten up and not be so serious. If you've been told you need to do this, maybe it's time to relax, to develop more of a sense of humor, and to not be so task-oriented when spending time with your spouse, family, and friends.

I'll sometimes ask a couple, "What do you do for fun?" In most cases, the response is the same: they'll look at each other, shrug their shoulders, and say, "I don't know, we don't have time for fun." How sad to think that there is no time to have fun in a marriage relationship. In some cases, not having a good time could be the source of a couple's problems.

Developing a sense of humor does not mean there needs to be constant humor in the relationship. We don't always have to tell jokes or be the life of the party. It does mean, however, that because there are so many negative pulls on a marriage relationship, looking for the humorous side can make situations more bearable.

Abraham Lincoln once said, "With the fearful strain that is on me night and day, if I did not laugh I should die."[2] To further illustrate the importance of humor, Thomas Carlyle wrote, "True humour springs not more from the head than from the heart; it is not contempt, its essence is love."[3]

AVOIDING NEGATIVE HUMOR

Humor should never be used to hurt others. When sarcasm is used, feelings and self-worth are usually damaged or destroyed. Sometimes individuals are so caught up in making a good impression, being the life of the party, or trying to positively influence other people that they become less sensitive to the reactions of the person who is the brunt of their stories.

From my experience, if a person is hurt or injured because of the "humor" of another, the humorous person needs to change his or her ways. The person being hurt is always right in his perceptions, even if he is being accused of being too sensitive or overreacting. Anticipation of how others might react to your humor is always important. Even though we may never intentionally hurt someone's feelings, we all need to develop self-awareness of how our humor is received.

Notes

1. J. Rust and J. Goldstein, "Humor in Marital Adjustment," *International Journal of Humor Research*, 2, Vol. 3, 1989, 217–23.

2. www.alincoln-library.com.

3. www.quotationsbook.com.

Infertility

Q: Ever since I was a little girl, I have loved playing with dolls. I loved dressing them up, taking them on walks, and just playing the role of Mom. I am now married, and my husband and I have decided that we want a large family because we both came from large families. After being married for three years and not getting pregnant, I finally went to the doctor. I just received news that because of some serious health problems I have, it will be impossible for us to have our own children. This is a total shock and extremely disappointing to us both. I'm on an emotional roller coaster. What do I do now?

Q: My wife feels like it's her fault we can't have children. What can I do or say to help her not feel guilty, and let her know I don't blame her and I still love her?

For some couples, the wish of parenthood is never granted. To others, it is granted after trying and failing many times. Some of the most devastated couples I have worked with over the years have been unable to conceive. To illustrate the inner feelings a couple can experience, I'll take excerpts from a letter given to me by a woman who, after many tests, was recently informed that she would not be able to conceive. With her permission, I share the following:

> You asked me the other day how I was and I gave the answer that I would give most people when they would ask, "Good." But after you asked me, I went to church on Sunday and the lesson was on the roles of women and the emphasis was on bearing and rearing children. I

don't know why, but I couldn't help getting emotional and I had to leave. During the following week I was fine. I look after a friend's baby twice a week and it doesn't seem to affect me at all. Then Sunday comes again and I see that there is a newborn baby at church, and the mother looks happy and her husband looks so proud. I feel sorry for my husband who loves me so much and is so supportive. I cry at times for what seems to be no reason. I think my husband doesn't like to see me cry and consoles me the best he can, but his answer is to not think about it. But everywhere I turn there is a reminder of what we may not ever have. The thing that doesn't seem to help are the statements such as "you can adopt," or "there are plenty of children that need good homes." Somehow it is not comforting to hear. Well, I just need to talk to someone and I feel comfortable letting you know. How can I overcome this and live so it doesn't affect me so negatively? Sorry for burdening you with this.

Most of us know couples in the same situation. It's very difficult to know what to say that would be appropriate and comforting. A variety of emotions are experienced with infertility—anger, despair, disappointment, guilt, sorrow, and blame. Even though there is no baby present, an infertile couple is suffering a death—a death of someone who has not yet been born, a death of what could be, and a death of what should be.

The biggest question is summarized in one word: Why? Of course, we know that there is no definitive answer that is acceptable. Finding out where the problem lies takes an enormous amount of patience, faith, and finances. Intrusive tests will need to be conducted so that a proper diagnosis can be made, followed by the appropriate treatment plan.

The infertile couples often ask why it's happening to them, what they did to cause it, and why two people who are so ready to be parents aren't being blessed. Couples always want to make sense of the situation confronting them. The problem is, they never come up with an answer they can feel good about. Scientifically, we might know why a couple cannot have children, but spiritually, peace may not come until much later.

If infertility is a part of your marriage, allow yourself time to mourn and grieve. Be patient with yourself. It is normal to feel depressed and negative, but know that those dark feelings of victimization can turn into feelings of optimism and opportunity. Fill that void with other meaningful activities. With God's help, peace and comfort will become a part of life again. This is best accomplished by acquiring a spiritual perspective and allowing God to influence your life.

The husband, even though disappointed himself, has to become even more compassionate and sensitive to his wife. He must not try to talk his wife out of her pain. He must empathize with her and avoid saying there must be a reason for this trial. This won't make her feel any better; she will only feel like he doesn't understand what she is going through. Instead, he should tell her that he knows how hard this is for her and that he is always there for her. She will know how understanding he is of her feelings, and appreciate his offer to help in any way. The husband must allow time for healing and have the faith that at some point, in spite of how his wife feels, life will get better.

During this emotional and perplexing time, it is extremely important for the couple's close friends and family members to be supportive and encouraging. It is not appropriate to give false hope or reassurance when unfounded. Even though there is a void in the couple's expectations, focus needs to be placed on their relationship, their employment, and other aspects of their life other than the infertility.

It is important for the couple to have an empathetic support system, rather than one that will try to talk them out of their grieving and mourning. It is normal to feel pain and disappointment during this time. However, mourning should not incapacitate them from conducting their normal daily activities.

And above all, it is important for the couple to support each other, no matter what the outcome of the situation is. There should be no blame, no criticism, and no anger projected on one person or the other. The partners should share their feelings of disappointment and despair.

Even though infertility is a major issue for some marriages, there are so many other aspects of the relationship that can be focused on and developed. Couples need to move ahead in their relationship in spite of their pain, not because of it.

Infidelity

Q: Since their marriage, Jake and his wife have grown into two very different people with different goals. Jake has been working hard to improve himself, while his wife is unmotivated and lazy. Jake works with a very dynamic woman named Dixie, who has many of the same goals and ambitions Jake has. Dixie is married to a successful businessman who gives her all she wants and needs, but he is always away on business trips. Dixie complains of being lonely and having little connection with her husband. Jake and Dixie have fallen in love and have made excuses to their spouses so they can see each other more. Would it be wrong if both Dixie and Jake could find some happiness together that they lack in their current relationships?

Q: Both my husband and I are religious. We were married in a church and the minister told us that if we kept the Lord in our marriage, it would be protected and we would be successful and happy. My question is this: is my marriage safe from mistrust and infidelity, or should I still be concerned about these issues?

Q: I'm afraid my spouse has been secretly seeing someone else. How can I talk about this suspicion without causing a huge fight?

Q: I would never leave my husband, because I believe in marriage. However, I often wonder what it would have been like if I had married someone else. I often find myself comparing my spouse to other men I know, wishing he possessed many of the qualities they possess. I work with a man named Bill, and sometimes I have fantasies about him. Is it wrong to have these kinds of fantasies, even if I know I'll never act on them?

Q: I love my wife but often find myself thinking about past relationships. I find myself often comparing my wife to other women I dated, and sometimes I make subtle references to these comparisons. However, now these comparisons have caused some tension in our marriage. What can I do to fix this?

Q: Recently, a good friend of ours has been struggling because he doesn't feel his wife listens to him. He and I are very alike in personality, and I've been able to help him by listening to his concerns. My husband found out about my conversations with this friend and is furious. Why does he think it's wrong, when all I'm doing is helping a friend?

Q: How can I justify breaking marriage vows and defiling marriage covenants, even though I am convinced I'm doing the right thing, and that the person I am involved with is someone I love enough to give up absolutely everything for?

Q: I have just learned that my wife is having an affair and no longer wants to be married to me. I never thought this could happen to us. I now have to ask myself some very thought-provoking questions. How much am I willing to do in order to save my marriage—if I can?

Q: Ed and Diane have been married for several years. Ed was often gone for business, and after one of his business trips, Ed told Diane that he has been involved with another woman. Ed isn't sure if he wants to try to continue to make his marriage work, or if he no longer wants to be married to Diane. Diane, although she too has mixed feelings, wants to be able to forgive Ed and continue on in their marriage. Ed and Diane have children, and Diane knows that her children need a father. Diane is also aware that how she speaks about Ed around their children can greatly influence the children's view of their father. Diane is unsure of how to make things work after all that has happened.

Q: I have been married to Tom for 11 years. I am trying to work my way up in the company and soon I will be up for the promotion that I have been anticipating. My boss recently suggested that he and I go out to lunch to discuss the details of the promotion. Should I go out with my boss to lunch and tell my husband beforehand, or should I wait and see if I'm even offered the promotion before I say anything?

Q: I was married in the temple, and my spouse and I did everything right to get there. I have been told that I am safe from the harms of infidelity in my marriage, because the Lord will protect our marriage if we keep all the promises and covenants we made. Am I truly safe from infidelity in my marriage, or is this something that I ought to still be concerned about?

The above questions are a small sample of many that could be asked about fidelity in marriage. Before beginning to address some of the specific concerns that these questions pose, let's take a moment to discuss a bigger picture.

Consumer-Pleasing Mentality

As mentioned earlier, we are a consumer-driven society. If the consumer is not happy for whatever reason with a particular product, he becomes entitled to return the purchased item. Most of the time, society has the attitude that the customer is always right. He knows that certain laws and norms are on his side so his rights can be satisfied. The frivolous lawsuits regularly mentioned in the news are a strong indication of this principle.

By the same token, if one of the spouse's needs is not met, he feels cheated since he has the right to have them met, and now can justify looking elsewhere to get them fulfilled.

Evolution of Infidelity

No marriage can handle a third partner. If the love between the couple is siphoned out to another person, the marriage will deteriorate over time.

Marriages are breaking up at an accelerated pace, and infidelity is occurring too frequently. It usually does not begin with adultery; it begins with thoughts, fantasies, justifications, and rationalizations. The steps toward adultery might begin simply and subtly, but once the process starts, it snowballs and becomes difficult to stop. Infidelity is easier to prevent than it is to repair. Affairs are more about emotional intimacy than physical intimacy. Infidelity doesn't make a bad marriage; it reveals a bad marriage. Don't let choices involving someone other than your spouse even get close to compromise.

When I talk to unfaithful husbands, I frequently hear, "I didn't plan for it to end like this." Or, "I never intended our relationship to go this far." Inevitably, what starts out as an innocent business meeting, luncheon, help with a personal problem, or support through a difficult time can end in tragedy.

Infidelity is usually an indicator of a marriage in trouble, and not the origin of trouble. The offending partner usually experiences emotions that haven't been felt with his spouse. The natural conclusion is that the current feelings are "the way things are to be," and he is missing out. The problem is that these feelings are viewed through a telescope, not binoculars; the feelings are distorting reality.

No matter what the state of your marriage is, it becomes very difficult to feel justified in staying married while carrying on with another person. It is not fair to the parties involved, and certainly not fair to any children that might be involved.

When the spouse first hears of the infidelity, some of the following questions are immediately contemplated:

- Do I throw him out?
- Will the affair stop?
- How long will it last?
- Can my marriage be saved?
- Should I talk to the spouse of the person with whom the affair happened?
- Will I ever be able to trust again?
- How do I get rid of my anger and ugly thoughts?
- Where did I fail?
- Will I ever forgive? Can I ever forget?
- Should I spy on my spouse?

STAGES OF DEALING WITH INFIDELITY

When infidelity has occurred, appropriate details should be shared with the spouse. This does not mean sharing the nitty-gritty details, but share enough to satisfy the offended spouse so he doesn't fill in the blanks himself. Such questions may be asked: How did it happen? Was it the act itself? How much time was spent with the other person? Was it the physical or emotional bond created between you two? If the couple cannot discuss how or why it happened and the feelings of hurt it created in the spouse, the indiscretion will most likely occur again.

The offended spouse needs to feel safe in expressing the variety of emotions he is dealing with. Sensitivity should be a major goal when exchanging information. It is essential that the emotions are processed to renew the commitment to each other and to the family. Partners sometimes need help from each other to make a thoughtful, not an emotional, decision about the process to recommit to the marriage.

Trust must be rebuilt in the relationship. This will take a great deal of patience and increased communication between the spouses. Obtain help for rebuilding trust, sexual intimacy, and learning to forgive. Understanding and patience will be necessary for this to be accomplished.

FLIRTATIONS

I have seen women who are jealous of their husband's outgoing and flirtatious personality. The husband usually responds to accusations by saying he is just friendly to everyone, and his actions need not be taken so seriously. However, flirtations are never harmless. Husbands need to be more sensitive to how their actions are perceived by their wives, and wives need to be sensitive to how their actions may be perceived by their husbands. If any behavior is causing stress to the relationship, it should cease immediately.

EMOTIONAL INFIDELITY

The answers to the following questions will help you know if you are having an emotional affair:

- Is your primary emotional gratification filled by someone outside of the marriage relationship?
- Are you more excited about spending time with your acquaintance than you are about spending time with your spouse?
- Is your marriage partner aware of the other relationship?
- Have you emotionally withdrawn from your spouse?
- Do you spend more time thinking about your "friend" than you do about your spouse?

- Are you lying, deceptive, or secretive to your spouse? Do offer excuses to your spouse when you spend time with your friend?

Because some men have not had physical sexual contact with another woman, they believe they have stayed true to their wives. Some of the most difficult cases I have dealt with involved an emotional affair, rather than a physical affair. What is an emotional affair?

- A person not only invests more of his emotional energy to someone else, but also receives emotional support and companionship from the new relationship.
- A person feels closer to the other party and sometimes even experiences increased sexual excitement.
- A person's emotional energy is limited and he or she is sharing intimate thoughts and feelings with someone else.
- Although cheaters are often guilt-free in an emotional affair because there is no sex involved, their spouses often view an emotional affair just as damaging as a sexual affair.
- Much of the pain and hurt from an emotional affair is caused by the deception, lies, and feelings of betrayal.
- A nonphysical friendship can evolve into an emotional affair when the investment of intimate information crosses the boundaries set by the married couple.
- An emotional affair is opening a door that should remain closed.
- One of the differences between a platonic friendship and an emotional affair is that an emotional affair is kept secret.
- The individuals involved in an emotional affair often have feelings of sexual attraction for one another. Sometimes the sexual attraction is acknowledged and sometimes it isn't.

Karen and Hank, both married, met while he was teaching a class at a local college. Karen was a student. After class, Karen would approach Hank and ask him for clarification on a particular point that he had made during the class lecture. As he was clarifying the point, students from the class that followed began coming into the room. To continue the clarification, Karen and Hank moved into the hallway, which soon became too noisy. They then moved to the cafeteria. The clarifications of class content occurred regularly week after week and soon, discussions evolved into exchanging information about their families and personal life. After some time, they both realized that they enjoyed each other's company and started to share the problems that they were experiencing in their own marriages. These conversations extended a few hours past the conclusion of class, and Karen felt that she needed to lie about her whereabouts to her husband. It was not long before her husband became suspicious. He began to secretly watch her after class and quickly realized what she was doing with her time. After a month of observing her behavior he confronted her and said, "Why are you spending so much time after class with the instructor?"

"I need help going over the class lecture," she replied.

"I think you have feelings for him. I've been watching you for over a month." He exclaimed.

"I do not have feelings for him. We are just good friends," she responded.

"As far as I know you might even be having an affair with him!" He shouted back at her.

"We are not having an affair," she angrily responded. "We have never even touched each other."

Was Karen having an affair? Some might think she was. Others might think she wasn't. Who is right?

The telltale sign of an emotional affair is happening "if your primary emotional gratification is outside the relationship and your partner is excluded," says Dr. Ann Langley, a marriage and family therapist. "If you're consistently going to your friend for the emotional nourishment that you're not getting from your husband, there's a good chance you're having an emotional affair."[1]

The verdict: It's not a crime to pal around with a friend of the opposite sex, but problems can arise if you emotionally withdraw from your spouse and if you spend most of your emotional energy on that friend.

"It's Just an Innocent Relationship"

You are married and there is a new male employee who has just been hired and is working in the cubical next to you. You discover over the course of a few weeks that he is not happily married, so the two of you begin talking about your marriage frustrations and problems. You find yourself fantasizing about what it would be if you were in a relationship with him. You find yourself thinking about him more and more.

Such a relationship may seem innocent, but if it affects the way you interact with your spouse when you get home, there is nothing innocent about it. According to Gary Neuman, "You know you've crossed the line if you come home and don't tell your spouse about your day because you're all talked out after sharing everything with your best same-sex friend"[2]

Rekindle the Spark in Your Relationship

1. **Have a weekly date night.** Get out of the house! Play tennis, take a walk, or check out a new local band. And while you're out, talk and get reacquainted with each other without talking about work, kids, or money.

2. **Get away together.** Since there are so many pulls on a couple for their time, effort needs to be made to get away together. This will take some advance planning and coordination, but it will be well worth the effort to get away, just the two of you.

3. **Reconnect with your spouse.** Because of infidelity, relationships have been greatly affected and even shattered. In order to mend them, you need to focus time and energy on your relationships. This will take a strong commitment. Planning ahead is vital. One-on-one time with children (if affected) is crucial.

In a national study of 777 individuals, Green and Sabini found that both genders showed more anger and blame over sexual infidelity, but more hurt feelings over emotional infidelity.[3]

In summary, be constantly on guard and protect your marriage relationship. If you do find yourself thinking more about someone else than your spouse, share those feelings immediately and get your marriage back on track.

Notes

1. "Is Your Crush Harmless? 7 Signs of Emotional Cheating," published 15 November 2006, www.lifescript.com.

2. M. Gary Neuman, *Emotional Infidelity: How to Affair-Proof Your Marriage and 10 Other Secrets to a Great Relationship* (New York: Crown Publishing Group, 2001), 50.

3. M. C. Green and J. Sabini, "Gender, Socioeconomic Status, Age, and Jealousy: Emotional Responses to Infidelity in a National Sample," *Emotion* 6 (2), 2006, 330–34.

In-Laws

Q: I think my marriage to Adam would be just about perfect if it weren't for his parents. Adam's parents seem to believe that all our decisions are really theirs. They've tried to tell us where to live, what to name our children, and where we should work. Adam is often swayed by his parents, and in many situations I think we would have been much better off if we hadn't listened to them. I don't want to burn any bridges with my in-laws, but they have been really intrusive in the past. How can I help Adam understand that his parents don't have the final say in all we do, and also help my in-laws understand that their advice isn't always welcome?

When couples begin their married life, they become a spouse more than a son or daughter. As such, the couple should cleave unto one another and work out difficulties on their own instead of always involving one or both sets of parents. This is a hard transition to make for some couples, but it is necessary.

Marrying your spouse means you turn your loyalties to him. That does not mean you are no longer loyal to your parents; rather, your spouse now becomes your number-one priority.

Now that the child is married, the in-laws need to disengage and allow the couple to grow and make mistakes together. The in-laws cannot control the marriage of the newly formed family.

It becomes essential for both the newly married couple and both sets of parents to be very sensitive to the amount of involvement that is permitted. This does not mean that assistance should not be given nor asked for. It does mean that the new in-laws should not try to control the married couple because of their wisdom, beliefs, or desires.

The obvious question is, "Does a relationship with a couple's in-laws have any effect on a marriage?" Research has shown that "even in long-term marriages, conflicts in extended family relations will erode marital stability, satisfaction, and commitment over time."[1]

COOPERATING WITH IN-LAWS

In-law problems can surface in different forms. Problems can arise between a married child and his parents, or between a married child and his in-laws, or a combination of both. Research shows that when in-laws are sources of conflict in a new marriage, the mother-in-law and the daughter-in-law are most likely the source of the problem.

Here are some tips sons- or daughters-in-law can use to minimize the possibility of difficulty:

- Seek approval for the marriage from your parents and your spouse's parents.
- When visiting with your partner's family, do it as a couple and make the experience a positive one for all concerned.
- Establish a dwelling apart from both partners' parents.
- Identify types of social and recreational activities that your new parents-in-law enjoy and try to find ways to enjoy some of the same types of activities.
- Address your new mother and father-in-law with affectionate titles. The closer to "Mother and Father" or "Mom and Dad," the better.
- Resolve to make your own decisions regarding schooling, finances, children, employment, and so forth. It's okay to ask for counsel and advice from parents and in-laws, but make sure you and your spouse make the final decision.
- When corresponding [with] or responding to your mother- and father-in-law, do it together as a unit or at least mention in the conversation that "we have talked it over and this is what we have decided."
- Remember that financial aid from in-laws often has strings attached. Know what strings, if any, there are and abide by those expectations or decline the aid.

- Find new ways to learn to appreciate your mother- and father-in-law.
- Refrain from telling mother-in-law jokes. Refer to your in-laws in positive ways.
- You will not be able to change your in-laws, so try to learn to love them as they are.[2]

Notes

1. Chalandra M. Bryant, Rand D. Conger, and Jennifer M. Meehan, "The Influence of In-Laws on Change in Marital Success," *Journal of Marriage and Family*, 63 (3), Aug. 2001, 614–26.

2. Adapted from Glen O. Jenson, "In-law Trouble Often Can Be Prevented with Cooperation," 21 July 2004, http://utahmarriage.org/htm/suggestions/in-law-trouble-often-can-be-prevented-with-cooperation.

Interracial and International Marriages

Q: My sister is dating a great guy, but he comes from a different racial and cultural background. They're planning on getting married in two months. I love my sister and I want the best for her. I think they'll be able to make their marriage work, but I'm concerned about some of the problems they'll face. What are some of the common problems people of interracial marriages face? How can they prepare for those challenges?

For the purpose of this chapter, the term "interracial marriages" will be utilized, while recognizing that in today's world, terms such as "interracial marriages," "intercultural marriages," and "international marriages" are used interchangeably, even though different dynamics can be associated with each descriptive term.

Every marriage requires commitment, dedication, and work. An interracial marriage requires even more attention because of the many challenges that a couple faces.

The purpose of this chapter is not to define interracial marriages as bad or good, or to explore the wide range of dynamics associated with interracial marriages. Nor is the purpose of this chapter to single out any particular combination of interracial marriages. Each interracial relationship has it own unique challenges, just as any marriage does. Regardless of what research says, each marriage has its own specific DNA and cannot be lumped into a general category. It is, however, the purpose of this chapter to point out that when an interracial marriage takes place, unique dynamics need to be considered.

Challenges from Others

As an interracial couple, you'll possibly face extra challenges from people outside your marriage. If you want to make sure these challenges don't hurt your marriage, talk about them with one another. Some of these challenges that others place upon you might include:

- Open hostility and intimidation
- Negative stereotyping
- Derogatory comments
- Stares, insults, jibes, slights, and whispers
- A sense of isolation
- Possible family rejection or being disinherited

Interracial Marriage Challenges

Some individuals may think it can be romantic and exciting to love someone who brings an element of diversity to the relationship. However, don't let the attraction of love distract you from dealing with the issues that an interracial marriage may include.

Don't believe the myth that your love for one another can overcome anything life throws at you. Every married couple needs to develop and use effective communication skills to deal with difficulties in a healthy way. An interracial couple needs to pay special attention to and discuss several things prior to marriage.

Focus on similarities: Even though there will be many differences in your marriage, there will also be many similarities. These may be things like expectations, goals, values, characteristics, and your love for one another. Since many differences will be pointed out to you throughout your marriage, you must always come back to the core beliefs and similarities that brought you together in the first place.

Children: You and your spouse need to discuss how you will raise your children and help them understand and appreciate their mixed identity. Make sure you provide your children with positive stories from both of your families' histories.

As your children grow up, allow them to share their concerns, doubts, and possible prejudices. Lovingly answer any questions they may have.

Holidays: All married couples face stress during holidays. Talk about your cultural differences regarding how holidays were celebrated when you were children. Realize that holidays give the two of you a chance to discuss how your family will handle both the differences and similarities in your backgrounds.

Be proud of your cultural traditions, and work together to create meaningful ways to celebrate them.

Know Yourself: Believe in who you are. If you're confused about your own life, deal with your issues before trying to merge your life with someone else's.

Know Your Differences: Each of you comes from different cultures and traditions. You must be knowledgeable of and sensitive to those traditions and customs such as religion, language, parenting practices, extended family relationships, and gender roles. Don't try to change the culture or traditions of your spouse. There must be plenty of give-and-take in this area. Do not view this as giving up or losing, but rather as acquiring additional ways to accomplish your goals and celebrate life events.

Conclusion: The racial and cultural differences in your marriage won't necessarily cause your relationship to fail. What can cause an interracial marriage to fall apart is the couple's inability to handle their differences, failure to talk about stress, and prejudice created by others.

INTERNATIONAL MARRIAGES

Mary Natali has listed the following common concerns that all couples entering into an international relationship should think about and discuss:

- In which country will you live?
- Whose culture will be dominant?
- What will the children's nationality be?
- What language will the children speak?
- What will the children's names be?
- What if you divorce?
- What happens if the spouse dies?[1]

"International marriage is not for the feint of heart. It requires its participants to look at the world in a different way, to change long-established patterns of behavior, to cope with the prejudices of two cultures, to learn new skills and a new language, and to be extra caring and understanding of a foreign partner. The global perspective that comes from living in a home built upon two cultures is a gift one can pass along to future generations."[2]

In an article entitled "What are the Strengths of Interracial Families?" Kelly N. Burrello lists the following strengths she found prevalent in interracial families that might be missing in non-interracial families:

- Many interracial families live in culturally diverse neighborhoods.
- Parents of multiracial children tend to preserve the richness of the customs and languages of both cultures.
- They teach their children about diversity and model appropriate behavior on how to treat those who are different.
- Parents teach their children to exhibit patience with those who ask them questions about being biracial. This includes keeping your cool, and not screaming at people who ask questions with negative overtones.
- Interracial families build bridges with their respective families by teaching them about both of their cultures. In addition, parents may demand grandparents to treat their children the same way they treat their other grandchildren.
- Interracial couples often agree on what they will tell their children when asked, "Who am I?" and "Where do I belong?"[3]

Conventional wisdom typically classifies a mixed-race child as being of the same race as the minority parent. "But that rule is being challenged as more interracial couples insist that their children be allowed to claim all sides of their heritage—an approach that experts think makes for a more settled, secure child."[4]

Statistics

The following statistics come from the 2000 census.

- Nearly 7 million (2.4 percent) of Americans described themselves as multiracial.
- Among Americans younger than 18, for example, 4.2 percent were multiracial, compared with 1.9 percent of adults.
- Census officials claim that the number of interracial couples more than quadrupled between 1970 and 1995.
- Among the 13 states where the Census Bureau has released detailed race information so far, multiracial populations range from less

than 1 percent in Mississippi to 4.5 percent in Oklahoma.

- Thirty years ago, only 1 in every 100 children born in the United States was of mixed race. Today that number is 1 in 19. In states like California and Washington, it's closer to 1 in 10.[5]

Stanford University sociologist Michael Rosenfeld calculates that more than 7 percent of America's 59 million married couples in 2005 were interracial, compared to less than 2 percent in 1970.[6]

In their book, *Establishing and Maintaining Satisfaction in Multicultural Relationships*, Gaines and Brennan emphasize the following:

1. During the formation of multicultural relationships, satisfaction is promoted to the extent that partners genuinely appreciate, rather than simply tolerate, the differences in their respective personalities.

2. After multicultural relationships have been formed, satisfaction is maintained to the extent that partners jointly create and sustain relationship cultures that are uniquely theirs.

3. Throughout the development and maintenance of multicultural relationships, satisfaction is created and sustained to the extent that relationship partners are open to personal growth via their association with a partner who contributed to their growth, in part due to being from a different culture/ethnic group.[7]

In today's world, it is important to become more culturally sensitive and tolerant of differences, including interracial and international marriages. Segregation as we knew it forty years ago no longer exists. Liberalizing one's views about interracial marriages is a necessity in today's world, since these unions are around all of us. It's necessary for one to become more accepting of mixed marriages, even if it would not be appropriate for himself.

As in any marital relationship, individuals in interracial marriages have to make adjustments. Before marrying, ask your future spouse about his culture, and become as fully aware of it as you possibly can.

Notes

1. Mary Natali, "Interracial Marriages," *Transitions Abroad Magazine*, Jul./Aug. 2001, http://www.transitionsabroad.com/publications/magazine/0107/international_marriages.shtml.

2. Ibid.

3. Kelly N. Burrello, "What Are The Strengths of Interracial Families?" http://www.diversitydtg.com/.

4. Blackmon, et. al., "Multi-Colored Families: Racially Mixed House-holds Face Their Own Challenges, Hear How They Are Trying to Meet Them." *Time,* v153, i17, 1999, 80A. As quoted in Burrello, "What Are The Strengths of Interracial Families?"

5. *Newsweek,* 8 May 2000, as quoted in Burrello, "What Are The Strengths of Interracial Families?"

6. Michael Rosenfeld, as quoted in Associated Press, "Interracial mar-riage flourishes in U.S.," 15 Apr. 2007, http://www.msnbc.msn.com/id/18090277/.

7. Stanley O. Gaines, Jr., and Kelly A. Brennan, "Establishing and Main-taining Satisfaction in Multicultural Relationships," *Close Romantic Relationships: Maintenance and Enhancement,* John H. Harvey and Amy Wenzel, eds., (New York: Psychology Press, 2001), vii.

Intimacy

Q: My wife and I have been struggling with some intimacy difficulties for the past few months. I haven't been as satisfied with our relationship, but I don't feel like I'm able to talk about these things with my wife for fear that it will hurt her feelings. How can I create a deeper emotional bond with my wife and improve our intimacy?

Q: We are having trouble with our physical intimacy. We are not currently trying to conceive a child, but how do we know when we should see a doctor or therapist about our problems?

Q: Gary and Lorraine feel like they are slowly growing apart. They have been struggling to improve the intimacy in their marriage, but seemingly to no avail. Lorraine would like to get some outside help, but she isn't sure Gary will consent to go with her.

Physical intimacy is an important part of the marriage relationship. If there are physical conditions preventing the close bond that should be achieved, please see a specialist.

Men often think that a good sexual relationship will create a positive marriage. Women believe that a strong marriage will create a good intimate relationship. Who is right?

Few couples I have seen needed sex therapy because of lack of skill. Both partners are new to this physical intimacy in the beginning of marriage, so sensitivity, communication, trust, and patience will go a long way in fulfilling each other's needs. Problems with intimacy are usually symptoms of other problems in the marriage, rather than the actual source of the problems.

To illustrate, I worked with a couple whose physical relationship had not been going well for the last three months. This was of great concern to them, because previously they had enjoyed this aspect of the marriage very much. Lately, the wife had no interest in physical intimacy; in fact, she felt repulsed by any advances her husband made. He was of the opinion that it was her obligation to be available when he desired. When she refused, he would verbally attack her, calling her names and insulting her. This did not motivate her, but rather distanced her even more. During the first interview, it was evident that their problem was not intimacy itself; it was about holding grudges and feeling resentment about recent events in their marriage. When the past issues of resentment were vented and resolved, the physical aspect of their relationship dramatically improved.

It would be wrong to conclude that all intimacy problems in marriages are results of suppressed resentment toward the spouse. However, it would be correct to conclude that when there is difficulty with intimacy in the marriage, other problems in the relationship most likely exist. Remember, feelings not talked out have to be acted out. Intimacy is one area where a spouse can shut down and get back at his spouse by withholding affection.

Love

Q: I am so in love with my husband! We married three months ago, and life as a married person has been fun. I can't imagine that we could ever fall out of love, but I am concerned. Recently I have seen several of my friends separate from their spouses and later get divorced. I don't want this kind of tragedy in our marriage; I don't want to become a statistic. What can we do to keep the love alive in our marriage?

Q: My wife and I just had our first baby. We are so excited about having this new little one in our family, but our marital relationship seems to have really taken a nosedive. We don't spend as much time together as we used to, and often the baby's needs and wants seem to come between us and our needs as a couple. What are ways that we can keep the love in our marriage burning brightly—even with a new baby?

Q: My wife and I have been married for several years. But lately it seems like my wife and I are living parallel lives. We live together, we see each other daily, and we sleep in the same room; however, as life has gotten busier and busier, we have begun to grow apart. We don't seem to have that much to talk about, and the awkwardness is sometimes so great that we occasionally avoid being around one another. We are comfortable with being married; however, the love and excitement we once felt for each other seems to decrease all the time. Neither of us has committed any major sins, but there isn't much excitement in our relationship anymore. We have decided we need some extra help to improve our relationship, but we aren't sure which direction to take.

How can we rekindle the love we once had?

These three questions all have something in common: fear of losing the love and excitement that initially existed in the marriage relationship. Whether it is an anticipatory fear or one that has come to pass, something needs to be done to change the direction in which the relationship is headed.

KEEPING LOVE ALIVE

As simple and trite as it sounds, keeping love alive in a marriage relationship takes constant effort. Spouses can never take each other for granted. Time always needs to be created so that the relationship between husband and wife remains paramount. There will always be various "pulls" to take away time and energy from the couple, but with constant effort and adjustments, the relationship can remain vibrant and meaningful.

A research study by John Gottman illustrates the importance of keeping love alive in the relationship after a new baby enters a couple's life. Gottman and his associates followed couples from the beginning months of their marriage through the transition stage of parenthood. The pool consisted of 43 couples who became parents, and 39 childless couples (the control group). Gottman found the following:

"What predicted the stable or increasing marital satisfaction of mothers were the husband's expression of fondness toward her, the husband's high awareness for her and their relationship, and her awareness for her husband and their relationship. In contrast, what predicted the decline in marital satisfaction of mothers were the husband's negativity toward his wife, the husband's disappointment in the marriage, or the husband or wife having described their lives as chaotic."[1]

It can be concluded from this research study that it is extremely important for each spouse to have a high degree of awareness and sensitivity toward the other. When that sensitivity declines, disappointment and resentment creep into the relationship. Doing the little things in a relationship does mean a lot. The following quote illustrates this point:

> Hollywood has dramatically distorted our notions of romance and what makes passion burn. Watching Humphrey Bogart gather teary-eyed Ingrid Bergman into his arms may make your heart pound, but real-life romance is fueled by a far more humdrum approach to staying connected. It is kept alive each time you let your spouse know he or she

is valued during the grind of everyday life. Comical as it may sound, romance actually grows when couples are in a supermarket and the wife says, "Are we out of bleach?" and the husband says, "I don't know. Let me go get some just in case," instead of shrugging apathetically. . . . I know there's deep drama in the little moments.[2]

Most couples know what they need to do in order to make their marriage better, but they sometimes don't feel like doing those things. If we do the right thing before we feel like doing it, the desire will come. Love is as much a verb as it is a noun. Saying "I love you" is much more a promise of behavior and commitment than it is an expression of feeling.

The earlier a couple recognizes that their marriage is growing stale, the better their chance is for a full recovery. Couples can do a number of things to mend their marriage and recapture the excitement of earlier times. Charles Beckert has offered the following techniques for showing love within a marriage:

- **Do what works.** Do not let the simplicity of this strategy make you doubt it.
- **Speak the language of love.** Another old and reliable technique for keeping love alive in marriage is to tell your spouse, at least once a day, how much you love and appreciate him or her. But say it in the language your spouse understands best. Some of us like words, some appreciate actions, and some respond best to touch. Discover and use your spouse's love language.
- **Touch to say hello and good-bye.**
- **Look for the good.** Don't be a faultfinder, be a "good" finder. Negativism and criticism create distance between two people; being positive and complimentary creates closeness.
- **Avoid the discouraging word.** Using words of encouragement, love, respect, courtesy, appreciation, admiration, and gratitude as we talk with one another will motivate us to spend more time together.
- **Smell the roses.** Wise couples find a few minutes each day to ponder the blessings of their marriage—its potential for eternity, how much they appreciate each other, and so forth.
- **Experience the wonder of the weekly date.**
- **Render "due benevolence."** Benevolence would include such behaviors as respect, courtesy, kindness, and generosity. What a

wonderful blessing a marriage can be when we treat each other with love.[3]

FIVE GOOD IDEAS

1. Make the effort to find out more about your spouse's job or activities at home.
2. Explore new ways to help. Husbands, if your wife is primarily responsible for the care of the home, find out what you can do to help with the load. Wives, if your husband isn't the kind to speak up about the pressure he's under at work, find a way to lend your listening ear and let him know you're concerned.
3. Think about how your spouse's talents and strengths might be used in service to others.
4. Make time to talk about things other than children or family finances.
5. Study the scriptures together.[4]

To again emphasize the point that little things mean a lot in the marriage, Joyce K. Fittro indicated:

> In researching what creates satisfaction in a marriage, one of the most significant findings was expressing affection on a regular basis. In other words, the couples who indulged in frequent terms of endearment, nonsexual touching, such as hugs and pats on the head, and tokens of affection, such as little gifts, reported extremely high levels of marital satisfaction . . . [Couples] think the candy and flowers, the sweet nothings, the silly names, are just a prelude to a real relationship. On the contrary, they light up your relationship.[5]

The authors then provided a list of things that would help couples revitalize their marriage:

- Start each day with a big hug.
- Send a card or love note to your spouse.
- Telephone to say "I love you" during the day.
- Give the gift of listening: refrain from judging or giving advice.
- Complete daily chores together and let this time become special sharing time.
- Put on a slow song and dance before retiring for the evening.
- Give your spouse a list of ten terrific memories.
- On a clear evening, share a brief stargazing experience.

- Assure your spouse often that you care, and show you care by how you act.
- Thank your partner for compliments and kind gestures—and you'll get more of them.
- Help without being asked.
- Always take each other's feelings into consideration.
- Make having fun together a priority.
- Look for the good in your partner and praise it.
- Admire each other's achievements.
- During tough times, think of why you fell in love in the first place, and dwell on those things.
- Always make your partner feel special.
- List all the ways your partner enriches your life, and share your list with your spouse.[6]

In a recent journal article by Volf Miroslav of the Yale Divinity School, we read that "Love between partners is a sparkle in the eye, a warm feeling. It [love] has to do with how you treat each other when dishes need to be washed or garbage taken out, when misunderstandings arise and when one has transgressed against the other. Love is not [just] the desire to be united with the other, but action on behalf of the other, and constancy in pursuit of his or her well-being."[7]

It's not the big acts of kindness, but rather the quiet moments that mean the most. They show concern. They demonstrate devotion. They manifest a focus of attention on your partner, which never goes unappreciated.

KEEPING LOVE ALIVE AFTER THE FIRST BABY

It's hard enough to adjust from thinking about yourself to thinking more about your spouse after you get married. The time it takes for that adjustment to take place varies from couple to couple.

Just when you and your partner think you have all the kinks worked out, you discover your wife is expecting. This is a time of excitement and planning for the new addition to the family. Of course, for years you've been told that having a child will be time-consuming, but that would happen in the future. Now it is staring you right in the face. For months you've had to think only about the two of you, as if that weren't a big enough adjustment to make. But you love each other, and the adjustment to the new baby will be a joy.

When the new baby arrives, she becomes the main focus of your relationship. Each of your needs, desires, and wants are placed in a secondary position—the baby comes first. You have to adjust to the added excitement, adventure, new experiences, frustration, pressures, time limitations, and of course financial obligations. Again, every waking minute revolves around the new little baby.

It's difficult to go on a spur-of-the-moment date anymore. In some instances, the couple is too tired to even plan a date. It's next to impossible to go away for a weekend and leave the baby behind. Even going out for dinner and a movie takes much planning with diapers, formula, the car seat, and so forth. Sometimes, you'll make plans and hire a babysitter, and then you'll have to cancel everything because of some complication with the new baby. Having a new baby in the home is extremely time-consuming. At the end of the day, instead of sitting down and discussing the events, both parents, especially the mother, are too tired to carry on a meaningful conversation.

Careful planning and sensitivity to the time and energy invested in the marital relationship are extremely important. You still need to go on dates. They may need to be modified, but dates are necessary. Time out from caring for the newborn is also needed; do not neglect each other.

Feelings of neglect may easily surface. The new father should not play the role of martyr. It is easy for him to feel neglected because the baby takes some of the attention he previously received from his wife. It does no good for the couple to blame each other for the lack of attention. In almost all cases, the spouse is not neglected intentionally; it's simply a case of spending time and energy with the new child.

Q: My son has married a beautiful, wonderful girl. However, I am concerned that he is not treating his wife with the respect she deserves. How can I convince him that he needs respect his wife more?

Marital love based on the notion that people should give their spouses and children the love, respect, and affection they expect for themselves (the golden rule) will help to improve marriages and family life.

Providing love and respect for the spouse, separate from obligations or benefits to the self, is a strong predictor of marital satisfaction. This can usually be demonstrated by being emotionally and sensitively available to each other, as you were during your courting days. Remember that your spouse is not only your spouse, but your friend.

FRIENDS

True friends are like jewels
So precious and rare
They comfort and bless you
With their love beyond compare.

God sent you, my friend
To bring joy to my life
And so I have been blessed
By your love without end.

Another precious gift we share
Is our knowledge of God's plan
That as friends and sisters we'll be
Throughout all Eternity.[8]

—Ruth R. Stringham—

REKINDLING LOVE

I once worked with a couple who were very angry with each other, and divorce seemed imminent. No issue discussed was resolved. They were always angry, frustrated, and irritated with each other. It was evident that each was disappointed in the other for not being sensitive to individual needs and fulfilling them.

As I continued to work with them, I noticed that each was blaming the other for their unhappiness. During the course of our sessions, the focus began to change from altering the other spouse to first changing the self. They initially received this change of focus with much hesitation, because both were convinced that the pain they felt was not caused by them, but by their spouse.

I believe in the adage that if you want to have a better marriage, you change yourself first, and then the marriage will improve. The couple mentioned above became more aware of themselves and their limitations and the impact those limitations had upon the marriage. Their marriage began to improve within weeks, and the feelings of love and tenderness that had been absent for so long began to return. I did not use any specific theory or technique; rather, I assisted each person individually in strengthening his weaknesses in the relationship. As we improve ourselves, we are more capable of reaching out to others without any expectation of reciprocation.

Love is how you treat others when stress is present: when floors need to be cleaned, carpets need to be vacuumed, dishes need to be washed, garbage needs to be taken out, or misunderstandings arise and one has been short with the other. Love is more than the desire to be together; it is the things we do for and in behalf of our spouse; it is constantly looking out for our spouse's welfare.

It is important to see the word *love* as a verb rather than as a noun. Then, saying, "I love you," will be an ongoing demonstration of action and service, not just an expression of feeling. *Feeling* love for someone is not nearly as important as *showing* love to someone.

Q: I recently went to a marriage seminar on "love currencies," which is showing your spouse love in a way that is most meaningful to him. For example, some people like to be told "I love you," others like to be touched, and others prefer a combination of both. I learned that we all like to be shown love in different ways. How can I find out what my spouse's love currency is?

Ask him! Discuss which actions make you each feel the most loved. This may be something you have not fully examined. If so, then it becomes your opportunity as a couple to figure out what your spouse's love currency is.

You can start by asking questions like these:

- How do you know when I love you?
- What actions, words, or instances/experiences prove to you that I love you?
- What things would you like me to do to show my love?

However, you probably already know certain things they like. Maybe it's a hug, a kiss, or saying "I love you." Think about it: what have you done that they like? What do you do when you want to win them over? Do they like their back scratched? Do they like flowers or phone calls? Chocolate? A surprise weekend getaway?

There's more here to address than just someone's love currency. You need to have a desire to express love to your spouse and put forth the effort to remind him constantly of the love you have for him. If you have no desire to show love, expressing it becomes very difficult.

FORCING LOVE

One of the biggest problems I see is one partner putting pressure on the other to love him. He does this in a variety of ways, with the most common being guilt. The husband might say to the wife, "You know we can't get a divorce; it would be too devastating to the children." Or, "You know you won't find anyone better than me." You can't make someone love you by using guilt or logic.

A lady once asked me if I would see her two children, ages eight and ten, in counseling. When I asked why, she responded with, "Their father and I are getting a divorce, and I want you to make them feel good about it." I told her I couldn't do that. I could see them and provide a safe place for them to express their feelings, but I couldn't force them or tell them how to feel about the pending divorce.

Love is a basic requirement for a successful marriage. It cannot be forced or pressured. For a person to love another, love has to be freely given and received. Love has to be nourished, and each partner needs to be constantly reminded of the other's love. Frequent expressions of love, both through verbal communication and through actions, are vital for happiness in marriage.

Notes

1. A. F. Shapiro, J. M. Gottman, and S. Carrére, "The baby and the marriage: Identifying factors that buffer against decline in marital satisfaction after the first baby arrives." *Journal of Family Psychology*, 14 (1), 2000, 59–70.

2. John M. Gottman and Nan Silver, *The Seven Principles for Making Marriage Work* (New York: Three Rivers Press, 1999), 79–80.

3. Charles B. Beckert, "The Pitfalls of Parallel Marriage," *Ensign*, Mar. 2000, 22.

4. Ibid.

5. Joyce K. Fittro, "Making the Most of Your Marriage," http://utahmarriage.org/htm/suggestions/making-the-most-of-your-marriage.

6. Jerri Wolfe, *21 Ways to Reconnect as a Couple.* (Minneapolis: Family Information Service, 1992), as quoted by Joyce K. Fittro, "Making the Most of Your Marriage."

7. Miroslav Volf, "Married Love," *Christian Century*, Vol. 119 (12), 2002, 35.

8. Ruth R. Stringham is a relative of the author, and shared this poem with him through personal correspondence.

Marriage Destroyers and Myths

Q: I see so many married couples who aren't really happy. They seem to just exist. I don't want my marriage to end up like so many I see around me. What are some of the common traps that lead to unhappy marriages, and how can my spouse and I avoid those traps?

THE BEGINNING

On their wedding day, couples can't imagine not being in love. However, as stated earlier, 50 to 67 percent of marriages will end in divorce. Research indicates that the two most vulnerable times for divorce are during the first two years and after twenty years of marriage. Logically it can be concluded that a couple gets married and struggles to make the necessary adjustments, but after many months realizes their efforts are in vain, and gets divorced. Other couples realize they have problems in their marriage and will say to themselves, "Let's just stay together for the children, and after they leave the home we'll get divorced."

What happened to the love the couple once had? Did it just leave? How long did it take to leave? Could this decaying of the relationship have been prevented?

I have categorized and listed various behaviors and thought patterns into one heading called "Marriage Destroyers." These are ways in which spouses are inconsiderate of each other's feelings and behaviors. If they are present in your relationship, they need to be corrected. Most marriages might have a few of these destroyers present, yet they would consider their marriage "good." However, if more than a few of these destroyers are present, you may want to alter some of the patterns.

When a person resorts to a marriage destroyer, he does more than fail to get what he needs. The love, respect, and caring between the spouses is shattered. Usually a spouse will become unhappy, resentful, and mistrusting, which will then lead to withdrawal and disconnectedness in the marriage relationship.

MARRIAGE DESTROYERS

Please review the following list and evaluate whether some apply to your marriage. If any of them do, do all in your power to remove them from your marriage.

- Always maintaining that you are right, even when you do not have all the facts.
- Discounting or ignoring your spouse's feelings.
- Never apologizing, even when you are proven wrong.
- On the occasions when you are right, constantly reminding others.
- Believing that if your partner really loved you, he should know what you are thinking, feeling, and what your needs are without you having to mention them.
- Losing the desire to serve each other; taking your spouse for granted and no longer working to maintain closeness and romance.
- Always fulfilling your own desires and needs first, and then focusing on your partner's.
- Only seeing your spouse's weaknesses, and becoming critical of him and attacking him.
- Never admitting hurt, pain, or weakness; rather, immediately expressing your emotions in anger.
- When frustrated, identifying all of your partner's character flaws or family secrets and using them to make your point after a logical approach has failed.
- Using guilt to manipulate, get your own way, or punish your spouse.
- Becoming proficient at catching your partner being weak, but never commenting when you catch him trying to improve.

- Holding onto the past and rehashing your version of events as often as possible.
- Always coming to major conclusions based on only a few facts.
- Finishing or interrupting your spouse's sentences; after all, you know what he is going to say before he even says it. Plus, you can say it more eloquently and succinctly, and what you have to say is more important than what your partner is trying to say.
- Frequently apologizing and making promises but continuing with your current disgusting behavior.
- Spending less time sharing spiritual thoughts and feelings, pursuing spiritual goals, and participating in religious activities together such as temple attendance, daily prayer, regular scripture study, and family home evening.
- Acting facetiously or being sarcastic so your partner never knows when you're being serious.
- Feeling emotionally closer to someone other than your spouse. Sharing intimate and personal thoughts and feelings with another that you should only share with your spouse.
- Failing to do things you know express love to your partner.
- Making excuses for your bad habits.
- Pretending you are interested in and understand what your partner is saying, even if you have no interest in or idea of the point he is trying to make.
- Believing that because you are married, you can say really harsh and cruel things, and then take them back later, because you feel your spouse will always love you and respect you.
- Assuming that if you don't cheat or abuse your spouse, he will interpret that to mean he is loved. Nothing else needs to be done to show your love.
- Believing you don't need to apologize since you haven't made any mistakes, and acting as if you have no problems and don't need to make changes. In addition, believing your spouse is the one who needs to make all the changes.
- Being loud, stubborn, unyielding, and obnoxious. This will show your spouse that you are right and will enable him to feel closer to you and provide a strong desire within him to meet your expectations.

- Dogmatically maintaining that you know your partner's motives better than he does.

OVERCOMING MARRIAGE DESTROYERS

Some special tools can help a husband and wife who are committed to breaking down the walls of resentment and mythical thinking, and overcoming barriers built on past unresolved mistakes and differences. The following are a compilation of ideas accumulated over the years that I have found helpful when assisting couples to empower their marriage and eliminate destroying influences.

Use positive affirmation. Too often our communication within the family is negative. We see mistakes or problems and repeatedly call these to the attention of our spouse (or children), while the good they do goes unnoticed. But, we can change the atmosphere in our homes by consistently telling our family, at least once a day, how much we appreciate something good they have done. It's a fact that whatever behavior you positively affirm, reward, or reinforce will be repeated. You can never do this too much.

Use "I" messages rather than "you" messages. This is much less confrontational and much more healing. If a husband comes home from work and wants dinner, it would be better for him to say, "I sure feel hungry," rather than, "Why do you always put dinner on late?" Often, "you" messages place blame, eliciting defensiveness and negative responses. "I" messages share important information about the speaker, not the listener, and are much more acceptable.

Agree to use time-outs. If you are having a discussion and either of you feels threatened, uncomfortable, or on the verge of giving in to temper, call for a time-out. At any time in a discussion or argument, either partner should be able to call a time-out and take a brief break to calm down and regain control.

Try scoring your wants. When you are faced with a difference of opinion, try using the following exercise. "On a scale of zero to ten, how badly do you want to go to that concert? I'm a two; what are you?" Your spouse may respond, "I'm a three. Sounds like neither of us is too interested. Maybe we can think of something else to do." But when your spouse is a nine on something and you are a one, you can either give him a gift of love and go along with what he wants, or you can suggest that you table it for later discussion. In the meantime, you can collect more data on the issue, or maybe you will both have a new perspective on the situation by the time you talk about it again. It's okay to see things differently, but you may need to give yourselves time and space to work through a resolution on an issue.

Make time for fun and play. We need frequent breaks with our partner for renewal, rebounding, and fence-mending. All work and no play can kill a good marriage. Fun and play could involve visiting friends; going to movies, plays, or concerts; staying overnight at a romantic spot; walking or jogging; taking a class together; or any other good thing that both partners enjoy.

Eliminate the negatives. Some people habitually look for the negative; they expect the worst and see the dark side of everything. But dwelling on the negative drives people away from and kills affection. Instead of looking for the worst in each other, marriage partners need to support and nurture each other, tackling problems and mistakes kindly and gently.

Be open to change. There may be a better way to do something. Be flexible. This was one of the key factors I found in a study of couples with successful marriages; the couples could easily adjust to and adapt to new situations and problems.

Focus on friendship. Do things for your spouse you might want him to do for you. Discuss interesting things with your partner. Be the one your spouse can turn to for consolation and a listening, non-judgmental ear. The years you have together on earth are years to enjoy each other and build a friendship that will last for eternity.

Focus on your physical appearance. Make sure you do your best to look neat, clean, and attractive. It may seem like a small thing, but most partners appreciate being around someone who is aesthetically pleasing. A caution should be noted here: Don't spend so much time on yourself that when completed, opportunities to interact with each other have passed. Also, don't try so hard to look your best that it looks like you are trying to either hide something or look twenty years younger than you are. Dieting and exercising to the extreme can have negative effects upon a person's appearance. Try to look natural and age appropriate.

Seek help from a counselor. If the two of you cannot resolve the contention between you, seek out a counselor to help you through your difficulties. If you had a broken arm, you wouldn't hesitate to seek out a doctor for treatment, and the health of your marriage is much more critical than a broken bone.

While none of the above suggestions may radically transform a relationship by themselves, all of them together can make a tremendous difference. Love is a decision and a commitment to action. It takes hard work, consistent effort, and a selfless attitude to have a loving, positive marriage, but you can make it happen. If the relationship is important enough, then any behavior to maintain and enhance it ought to become a priority.

Eliminating marriage destroyers and putting forth the effort to break down the marriage barriers will help the marriage stay alive. A husband and wife need to be committed to breaking down the walls of resentment and overcoming obstacles built on past mistakes.

MARRIAGE MYTHS

MYTH #1: There is a "one and only" person for me.

REALITY: If this were true, an individual could spend his entire life looking for the right person. When he thought he had found her and then discovered imperfections, he would keep looking. Some individuals receive special guidance when selecting a spouse, but most people don't believe in predestined love. Individuals have to do the choosing based on the best knowledge, counsel, and inspiration available to them.

MYTH #2: A good marriage will always be romantic.

REALITY: Virtually all relationships experience peaks and valleys. Sometimes, the realities of married life will often cloud over romantic feelings. Scott Peck, in his book *The Road Less Traveled,* stated, "The experience of falling in love is invariably temporary. No matter whom we fall in love with, we sooner of later fall out of love if the relationship continues long enough"[1] Just because the feelings of love are not *always* present does not necessarily mean there is a lack of love. Love is more of a choice than a feeling.

MYTH #3: Marriage will automatically make me happy.

REALITY: A marriage partner does not have the power or ability to *make* another person happy. A person's sense of happiness must come from deep inside himself. Happiness is a state of mind, not a station in life. Marriage has the potential of complementing individual happiness and well-being, but it cannot be the primary source.

MYTH #4: If we really love each other, that is sufficient reason to marry; everything else will fall into place.

REALITY: Marriage needs constant nurturing. Because of individual, societal, and environmental changes, marriage is always in a state of flux; it's a dynamic relationship rather than a static one. Constant sensitivity to one another's needs and continual adaptation to relational changes are necessary to keep love alive.

MYTH #5: My partner should intuitively know my needs and expectations.

REALITY: Regardless of a spouse's intelligence or personal strengths, he does not have the ability to read his spouse's mind. Needs and expectations for security, affection, emotional support, encouragement, or physical assistance often must be verbalized in clear language—sometimes repeatedly.

MYTH #6: Conflict means a lack of love.

REALITY: Conflict is inevitable, but it doesn't have to be damaging to the marriage relationship. Partners have different viewpoints and different feelings that are based on their background and previous experiences. Those differences do not mean that one partner is right and the other wrong; it just means they are not alike in every thought and feeling. When dealt with appropriately, conflict can be healthy for a relationship because ideas and new perspectives are introduced to each partner and to the relationship.

MYTH #7: I should feel totally competent as a future spouse before getting married.

REALITY: Couples who marry for the first time have no prior experience with marriage. The only experience they know is what they have seen or read about. Marriage is "on the job training." If an individual approaches marriage with an "I know everything there is to know about marriage, and I will do a great job" attitude, big problems await. However, if an individual approaches marriage with the attitude of "I'm new at this and will commit mistakes, but I am committed to do my best. I hope my partner will be patient with me," he will be more successful in his marriage relationship. Someone who feels totally competent as a spouse prior to marriage will do more harm than someone who is humble, submissive, and has a desire to learn.

Linda Waite and Lee Lillard conducted a study for the National Institutes of Health, and later compiled their research into a book called *The Case for Marriage*. They mention five myths about marriages that are common in American culture:

1. Divorce is usually the best answer for children when the parents' marriage is unhappy. Some research, according to Waite and Lillard, did show that in many cases, "staying together is the best solution if the marriage becomes unhappy."[2]
2. Marriage is about children. "Married men and married women live longer and more emotionally satisfying lives."[3]
3. Marriage is good for men and bad for women. This theory is based on information from a book that included information on women's positive experiences with marriage at the end of the book, rather than in the text.
4. Women are more likely to be abused if they are married. The literature shows that women are just as likely to be abused by boyfriends and men they live with.
5. Marriage is a private affair or just a "piece of paper." Marriage is a commitment that changes how people treat one another and how others treat them.[4]

If any of the myths about marriage still ring true to you, please look deeper into yourself and your values. Discover why you believe as you do. Discuss these myths with your spouse and be open to feedback.

Notes

1. M. Scott Peck, *The Road Less Traveled* (New York: Simon & Schuster, Inc., 1978), 84.
2. L. J. Waite and M. Gallagher, *The Case for Marriage* (New York: Doubleday, 2000), 4.
3. Ibid.
4. Ibid.

Needs

Q: My husband, Fred, can be so thoughtless sometimes. I've been
trying to improve our relationship by doing little things for him,
but he never seems to notice my efforts. It seems he's not even trying to
meet my needs, even when I try to meet his. I think he believes that my
actions are just my duty to make him comfortable and happy. I'm not
trying to be selfish, but I want Fred to also have the desire to meet my
basic needs.

REMEMBERING THE NEEDS OF OTHERS

Spouses need to develop self-awareness concerning how they come
across to their partner. In an emotionally tight-knit relationship such as
marriage, one's idiosyncrasies and blind spots are easily detected. If the
husband or wife is not aware of those areas, he or she will spend a considerable amount of time in denial or being defensive. There will also be
a lot of time spent on meeting one's own needs, rather than focusing on
the other's needs.

Newlyweds encounter a challenge to change their way of thinking
from "me" and "mine," to "us," "we," and "ours." For approximately
twenty years before marriage, a spouse has only had to think in terms of
himself rather than the feelings and concerns of another. Now married,
meeting the needs of a partner can and should become more important
than one's own desires and needs. Couples need to be constantly thinking
of their spouse's needs, which can be somewhat different for both men

and women. Putting the needs of your spouse ahead of your own can be difficult, but it's central to making a marriage successful.

TYPES OF NEEDS

The hierarchy of needs, developed by Abraham Maslow, states that when our basic needs are satisfied, we can then move up the hierarchy until a higher need is satisfied. I have summarized Maslow's hierarchy of needs and their relevance in a relationship into three main categories: physical, emotional, and spiritual.[1]

Physical: We all have the need for food, water, shelter, and so forth. These basic needs must be met and satisfied. When they are not, it is more difficult to rise to a higher level of fulfillment.

Emotional: Having emotional needs met is usually the force behind behavior. Having emotional needs met overrides right or wrong. All of us have done something wrong at some point in our life. Why? Prominent emotional needs are feeling important and significant, experiencing control and power, and having a sense of belonging and acceptance. The following illustrations will demonstrate how each works.

Significant/Important. I worked with a sixteen-year-old girl who, every time she went out with a specific seventeen-year-old young man, would end up having inappropriate physical involvement. Her parents were devastated because they felt she knew better. They forbade her from seeing the young man again. That kind of restriction created a lot of ingenuity on the girl's part so that she could continue to see this young man without her parents knowing. That's when I was called in to help. I asked the girl, "When do you know the situation between you two will become negative?" She responded by saying, "When we are through with the movie or eating, and he says, 'Let's go for a ride.' I know what that means." I then said to her, "What does he say to you?" She answered, "He tells me that I am special; that of all the girls he has dated, I am the most special; that he has plans for us being together." Emotionally, how was she feeling? The answer is obvious: important and significant. Having those emotional needs met was more important than her behavior being wrong.

Power/Control. It is important to have power and control over our lives. Parents want that over their children. How is this manifested? Do you know someone who always has to be right? Do you know someone who knows more than others? Someone who never apologizes because he never makes a mistake? Someone who falsifies information? These characteristics are typical of individuals who want power and control and want to be viewed as important and significant in the eyes of others.

Belong. Most like to belong to a club, an organization, or a group that conveys to others a sense of identity and belonging. Young children belong to a specific sports team and will wear their team T-shirt to school to show that they belong. Some individuals belong to a secret gang because it provides a sense of belonging to a powerful group.

I once worked with a young man who was caught shoplifting a five-dollar item. The ironic issue was, he had ten dollars in his pocket. When called about the matter, his father was very upset and couldn't figure out the logic of his son's actions. Later, it was discovered that the son was being initiated into a gang, and part of the initiation was to shoplift something from a store without getting caught. The emotional need to belong was more powerful than the logical thinking of what was right and wrong.

Spiritual: Teilhard de Chardin said, "We are not human beings having a spiritual experience; we are spiritual beings having a human experience."[2] Maslow would call this self-actualization; reaching one's potential and having inner congruence between behavior and values.

Using the above hierarchy of needs as the basis to evaluate marriages, it can be noted that most conflict and disagreement is based on the basic needs rather than the higher order needs. Generally speaking, when couples explain their problems to me, I can usually determine if a physical, emotional, or spiritual need is not being met. It would be difficult for a person to get outside of himself if he were spending most of his time focusing on the basic physical needs of his family.

THE ROLE OF SELF-ESTEEM

Some don't believe in the concept of self-esteem, but how one feels about himself plays a significant role in how his needs are met. One needs to ask himself, "Is my self-esteem based on others' opinions of me (external validation), or is it based on how I intrinsically feel about myself (internal validation)?"

To illustrate these two concepts, the following questions could be asked:

- Is a person who earns $100,000 per year better than a person who earns less than $50,000 per year?
- Is a person who lives high on the hillside, in a more expensive

house, better than a person who lives on the other side of the tracks, in a smaller, more humble home?

- Is a person who drives an extremely expensive car better than a person who drives a car that is twenty years old?

We as individuals get caught up in a lot of external validation, which is translated into the importance or dignity of the individual.

Some might believe that people with good self-esteem have it all together. But someone with healthy self-esteem should be characterized by his awareness of areas that need to be improved—this is a sign of psychological strength. Also, a person with a healthy self-esteem would be able to own up to his mistakes rather than constantly blaming or projecting failures onto others.

Q: Because of some recent events in my life, I have suddenly realized that I need to reevaluate what and who is most important in my life. I need to help my wife understand that I love her and want to care for her on all levels. I have always worked hard to support my family's physical needs and wants, but I haven't always been sensitive to my wife's emotional needs. Showing emotions is very difficult for me. How can I learn to be more mindful of my wife's emotional needs?

It's quite common for a husband not to show emotion. This typically occurs for one of three reasons:

1. Showing emotion was never modeled for him while he was growing up.
2. He doesn't know how to show emotion and doesn't see the importance of it.
3. He is afraid to try, for fear of failure and embarrassment.

Reread this man's question and notice that the husband was meeting the basic physical needs of his wife but falling short on meeting her emotional and spiritual needs. He has reached an important step by realizing this. Recognizing the problem and having the desire to change is much more effective in resolving marriage issues.

The best solution would be to ask the wife, "What can I specifically do today to meet your emotional needs?" The husband needs to do whatever his wife says. At the end of the day, he should again approach his wife and say, "How did I do in meeting your emotional needs today?"

Whatever she says is her reality and is true for her. The husband will need to continue the desired behavior the next day. Wives, be specific when describing behaviors; do not talk in generalities. You are the expert on your emotional needs. This is not a game; it's real life.

This process will probably get the husband out of his comfort zone, but it is important for him to work on meeting his wife's needs. Part of maturing in a marital relationship is realizing that your spouse's needs are not necessarily your needs. Just because something is not important to you does not mean it isn't important to your spouse. Doing something for your spouse simply because it is important to her is central for happiness in a marriage.

From my experience in counseling couples, if this approach is implemented, progress will be made toward an improved relationship, and feelings toward each other will become more positive.

IMPORTANCE OF MEETING YOUR SPOUSE'S NEEDS

A 27-item checklist of reasons for divorce was administered to 207 men and 230 women who divorced in the mid-1980s. The most frequently cited factors for divorcing were unmet emotional needs and growing apart, lifestyle differences or boredom with the marriage, and high-conflict demeaning relationships.[3]

Another study indicated that the three most common complaints in marriage were lack of communication, constant arguments, and unmet emotional needs.[4]

WHEN NEEDS ARE NOT MET

If a husband told his wife he was going out to a ball game with his friends instead of celebrating her birthday that night, his wife would naturally feel insignificant to him. The husband may feel like they can celebrate her birthday on another night, while his wife feels like she should be more important than his friends and a ball game. He is of the opinion that he doesn't need to celebrate events that are "contrived" (Valentine's Day, their anniversary, and so forth). He would rather show his wife that she is special every day, not just on a few specific days, a few times a year.

In this example, the husband must realize that thinking of another (his wife) means also anticipating and thinking like the she does and understanding how to fulfill her needs.

When needs are not met, one will withdraw, withhold, or disengage from his spouse. When this occurs, the following questions could be asked: "Can the wife still be happy in this marriage?" "How will the wife respond to the husband when her emotional needs are not met?" She will naturally feel hurt and probably even withdraw from her husband. This is her way of stating that she does not agree with his behavior. He is not nurturing their relationship; therefore, their relationship will begin to die.

Notes

1. Maslow, "A. Maslow's Hierarchy of Needs," en.wikipedia.org/wiki/Maslow's_hierarchy_of_needs.

2. As quoted in Richards and Bergin, *A Spiritual Strategy for Counseling and Psychotherapy* (Washington D.C.: American Psychological Association, 1997), 5.

3. Lynn Gigy, and Joan B. Kelly, "Reasons for divorce: Perspectives of divorcing men and women," *Journal of Divorce and Remarriage*, Vol. 18 (1–2), 1992, 169–87.

4. Lionel Finkelstein, "Psychoanalysis, marital therapy, and object-relations theory," *Journal of the American Psychoanalytic Association*, Vol. 36 (4): 1988, 905–31.

Positive Emphasis

Q: Michelle used to do so many little things for her husband, Darrin. She would put kind notes in his pockets and do other small things to surprise him. In the past few years, Darrin has been working really hard to make ends meet for their family. Darrin has been very stressed with work and seems to be more distant emotionally. Michelle has found that Darrin doesn't even notice or comment on the little things that she has been trying to do to surprise him. Michelle knows she wants to continue, but when Darrin never notices her efforts and rarely does anything in return, Michelle begins to feel resentful of the kindness she is showing.

Marriages are likely to suffer when we spend our time thinking about and focusing on what others appear to have that we don't. When we compare our spouse to someone else, focus on the weaknesses of our relationship to other couples' strengths, or dwell on all that makes us unhappy in our relationship, our marriage begins to erode.

In *Why Marriages Succeed or Fail*, John Gottman mentions that love and respect are the basic marital nutrients needed for successful marriages. He says that "contempt, perhaps the most corrosive force in marriage," can be minimized by showing more love and respect to your spouse.[1]

Gottman has also studied different styles of marital conflict in men and women. He distinguished the kind of conflict that can destroy a marriage from conflict that occurs within its bounds, and has proposed that a good marriage is best maintained by emphasizing the positive more than the negative. He suggests that the ratio be 5:1—five positive interactions will offset the impact of one negative interaction. Gottman provides the following specific ideas to emphasize the positive aspects of a couple's relationship:

1. Show interest
2. Be affectionate
3. Show you care
4. Be appreciative
5. Show concern
6. Be empathetic
7. Be accepting
8. Be humorous
9. Share your joy[2]

Gottman also made the following observations:

- Couples are more polite to strangers than to each other.
- Couples need to avoid these warning signs: arguing often, insulting each other, name calling, sarcasm, becoming silent, desiring to be alone, living as "married singles" (legally being married but living separate, individual, or parallel lives).
- If you have a good marriage and do nothing to make it better, it will get worse over time.
- Chores should be referred to as "ours," not "yours." Husbands doing housework makes for a better marriage.[3]

Remember, "In the strongest marriages, husband and wife share a deep sense of meaning. They don't just 'get along'—they also support each other's hopes and aspirations and build a sense of purpose into their lives together."[4]

The following poem illustrates the need to focus on the positive more than the negative:

WHICH ONE IS YOU?

"Two A's are good," the small boy cried
His voice was filled with glee.
His father very bluntly asked,
"Why didn't you get three?"

"Mom, I've got the dishes done,"

The girl called from the door.
Her mother very calmly said,
"And did you sweep the floor?"

"I've mowed the grass," the tall boy said,
"And put the mower away."
His father asked him with a shrug,
"Did you clean off the clay?"

The children in the house next door
Seem happy and content.
The same things happened over there
But this is how they went:

"Two A's are good," the small boy cried
His voice was filled with glee.
His father proudly said, "That's great!
"I'm glad you live with me."

"Mom, I've got the dishes done,"
The girl called from the door.
Her mother smiled and softly said,
"Each day I love you more."

"I've mowed the grass," the tall boy said,
"And put the mower away."
His father answered with much joy,
"You've made my happy day."

Children deserve encouragement
For task they're asked to do.
If they're to lead a happy life,
So much depends on you![5]

—Author Unknown—

Every marital relationship can improve by emphasizing the positive more than the negative. Don't wait until you feel like focusing on the positive before you start. Feelings are a result of actions and perceptions. We need to develop the habit of focusing on what we do have, not on what we don't have. If you do, the feelings will come.

The following story vividly illustrates the principle of focusing on the positive more than the negative:

> On November 18, 1995, Itzhak Perlman, the violinist, came on stage to give a concert at Avery Fisher Hall at Lincoln Center in New York City. If you have ever been to a Perlman concert, you know that getting on stage is no small achievement for him. He was stricken with polio as a child, and so he has braces on both legs and walks with the aid of two crutches. To see him walk across the stage one step at a time, painfully and slowly, is an unforgettable sight. He walks painfully, yet majestically, until he reaches his chair. Then he sits down, slowly, puts his crutches on the floor, undoes the clasps on his legs, tucks one foot back and extends the other foot forward. Then he bends down and picks up the violin, puts it under his chin, nods to the conductor and proceeds to play.
>
> By now, the audience is used to this ritual. They sit quietly while he makes his way across the stage to his chair. They remain reverently silent while he undoes the clasps on his legs. They wait until he is ready to play. But this time, something went wrong. Just as he finished the first few bars, one of the strings on his violin broke. You could hear it snap. It went off like gunfire across the room. There was no mistaking what that sound meant.
>
> There was no mistaking what he had to do.
>
> People who were there that night thought to themselves: "We figured that he would have to get up, put on the clasps again, pick up the crutches and limp his way off stage, to either find another violin or else find another string for this one."
>
> But he didn't. Instead, he waited a moment, closed his eyes and then he played with such passion and such power and such purity as they had never heard before. Of course, anyone knows that it is impossible to play a symphonic work with just three strings. I know that, and you know that, but that night Itzhak Perlman refused to know that. You could see him modulating, changing, re-composing the piece in his head. At one point, it sounded like he was de-tuning the strings to get new sounds from them that they had never made before. When he finished, there was an awesome silence in the room. And then people rose and cheered. There was an extraordinary outburst of applause from every corner of the auditorium. We were all on our feet, screaming and cheering; doing everything we could to show how much we appreciated what he had done.
>
> He smiled, wiped the sweat from his brow, raised his bow to quiet us, and then he said, not boastfully, but in a quiet, pensive, reverent tone, "You know, sometimes it is the artist's task to find out how much

music you can still make with what you have left."[6]

What a powerful line that is. It has stayed in my mind ever since I heard it, and who knows? Perhaps that is the way of life. Not just for artists, but for all of us.

So, perhaps our task in this shaky, fast-changing, bewildering world in which we live is to make music, at first with all that we have, and then, when that is no longer possible, to make music with what we have left.[7]

Authors Billingsley, Lim, and Caron mention the following ten positive ways to keep your marriage strong:

1. **Tell your spouse, "I love you."** Showing your love through your actions is meaningful and wonderful. But the words "I love you; I need you; I think you're beautiful (or handsome); I appreciate you; thank you" never grow old.

2. **Tell your spouse, "You are so great!"** Be specific: "You're so kind; you know just what to say; I admire the way you notice the beauty of sunsets and roses; you help me so much; you are such a good parent; you're one of the most intelligent people I know."

3. **Show affection for your spouse.** Kiss your spouse before leaving and after reuniting. Hold hands at the movies or while walking. Take turns giving each other back rubs and head rubs. Share a recliner while you watch TV. Sit on each other's laps. Help each other with those hard-to-reach buttons and zippers.

4. **When praying together, express gratitude for your spouse.** Ask God to help with that project or test or ache or sniffle. Seek guidance to help your marriage be strong and your love unfailing. Ask God to be a part of your marriage and to bless you with increasing love and appreciation for each other.

5. **Encourage each other rather than nag about mistakes.** Help each other with tasks and goals. Talk about what you want to do in your wildest dreams (go to Italy? return to school? learn to make lace or create a beautiful landscape?). Then talk seriously about making those dreams come true.

6. **Laugh together.** Share funny stories or jokes. Remember the overnighters you took without the children and the funny moments connected to them. Look at photos and remember good times. Do anonymous good deeds and laugh about the pleasant surprises you've caused.

7. **Cry together.** Talk about loved ones who've passed on, and remember the loving things they did. Remember touching moments—the birth of a child, the turning point when an illness or injury finally showed signs of healing, the spiritual moments that have made you grateful to be alive and together, or your wedding.

8. **Sacrifice for each other.** Do a chore the other spouse would usually do. Arrange for him or her to have a day off, whether that means a day at the golf course or a day at home alone. Make or buy a special treat for your spouse, even if you don't like that treat. Finish a task for your spouse, or talk him into resting and finishing it later if he is tired and frazzled.

9. **Remember why you got married.** Tell each other five things that you saw in your partner that caused you to love and want to marry him. Tell each other five things you see in your spouse that make you happy to be married now.

10. **Accept and respect each other as children of God.**[8]

Another research study focused on the historical overview of literature written about marital and family success and the criteria that contributes to building strong relationships. In studies conducted between 1953–2004 of long-term marriages, nine common themes were identified: permanence of relationship, love, sex, compatibility in personality, common interests, communication, decision-making, intimacy, and religion. Similarly, the common themes among strong families include communication, time spent together, religion, conflict management, and appreciation.[9]

When not recognized for performing the small acts, should the spouse continue with the gestures? On the other hand, do you as the receiver express gratitude, or do you take these things for granted, assuming that it's just his "job"? Continue performing small acts of kindness because it's the right thing to do. If you don't receive positive validation from your spouse, keep doing these acts of kindness anyway.

On the other hand, each partner should be engaged in doing the "little things" to keep the relationship vibrant and fresh. When noticed, the receiver of the gestures needs to recognize these things and sincerely thank the giver. Do not respond by saying, "Thanks, but is that the best you can do?" Always reward the effort that someone makes to meet your needs and expectations, even if they don't completely meet them.

Recognizing the effort of another goes a long way, and the act is more likely to be repeated.

Notes

1. John M. Gottman, *Why Marriages Succeed or Fail* (New York: Simon & Schuster, 1994), 61–66.

2. Ibid., 59–61.

3. Ibid., 61–70, 155–57.

4. John M. Gottman and Nan Silver, *The Seven Principles for Making Marriage Work* (New York: Three Rivers Press, 1999), 23.

5. Author unknown. Poem retrieved from: www.memphisdyslexia.org/articles/poem.pdf

6. Jack Riemer, "The 390th Memorial Museum Foundation," *Houston Chronicle,* Vol. VII, No. 1, Spring 2002.

7. "The Family Files: How Much Money," *Marriage & Families,* Jan. 2002, 21.

8. S. Billingsley, M. G. Lim, and J. Caron, "Historical Overview of Criteria of Marital and Family Success," *Family Therapy,* 32 (1), 2005, 1–14.

Prayer

Q: My wife and I have been faced with several difficult decisions over the past few months. We have been caring for our aging parents, as well as dealing with the stresses of a growing family. After we pray, we honestly don't feel any different or receive a direct answer to our pleas. How can we be inspired to make the best choices possible when we aren't receiving any definitive answers?

Prayer can bring spiritual guidance in the form of a new idea, an impression, a feeling, or a direct answer to a specific question. It will usually be a quiet, peaceful experience. When you have that experience, it is imperative to anchor yourself with the impression and avoid logically explaining it away. Sometimes solving marriage problems is that simple. Of course, not all difficulties are instantly resolved with a few prayers. But prayer can change our attitudes and help us become more willing to work with each other.

Prayer eases tensions in amazing ways. Problems aren't inevitably solved when you get up off your knees, but when you pray, you invite the Lord into your life. As you become humble and recognize your need for help, the result is usually a change in your relationship. Specifically asking the Lord to help you use the resources and abilities you already have, and having the desire to search for and develop new ones, can really make a difference in your success. Prayer can bring a feeling of peace, and although peace doesn't by itself eliminate most challenges, it can help you work together to solve your problems, endure your problems better, or recognize that a resolution will come in its own due time. Peace can also give you the emotional room to find other answers. Some matters simply take time and continued effort to work through.

The importance and power of prayer was pointed out in a research study of 217 religious spouses. Researchers found that spirituality and spiritual practices emerge largely as positive predictors of individual and relationship outcomes. It was also noted that for religious couples, Deity's influence in their marriage is often invoked and experienced through prayer, and Deity may more regularly and significantly influence religious couples' interaction than anyone else, including family members. Participant spouses noted relationship softening, healing perspective, and perception or change of behavior as significant effects associated with their prayer experience.[1]

In summary, a benefit from prayer is feeling better about each other or about a specific complexity in the relationship, which, in turn, can help you find ways of overcoming the dilemmas facing the marriage, and gaining the confidence to make important decisions. Even if no definitive answers are received after praying, follow your intuition and integrate those characteristics into your marriage that you both think will help. They will be right for you, and your marriage will improve.

Notes

1. M. H. Butler, J. A. Stout, and B. C. Gardner, "Prayer as a conflict resolution ritual: Clinical implications of religious couples' report of relationship softening, healing perspective, and change responsibility," *American Journal of Family Therapy*, 30 [1], 2002, 19–37.

Priorities

Q: My schedule and my life seem to be so demanding lately. I know my marriage should be one of the top priorities on my list, but it seems like the demands for my time are always pulled by a million other tasks. It's hard for me to balance my time between my personal life, career, church, marriage, and family because they can all take every minute of my time each week. How can I better balance my time?

CHOOSING BETWEEN PRIORITIES

There are many things to accomplish in life and many demands on our time. Life in today's world is very demanding on everyone. There are so many priorities, so many pressures from things that need to be done, so many crises, and so many seemingly important things that all demand our attention. If all of these demands are good things, which ones does a person focus on? I refer to the many demands placed upon us, and ultimately the one that we choose to give attention to as "selective neglect." Whatever is decided is being done at the exclusion or neglect of other important items. Our marriage should not be viewed as interfering with other important aspects of our life; rather, these other aspects of our lives should be viewed as interfering with our marriage relationship, which is our first priority. Each partner needs to ask himself, "How much time and energy am I willing to put into my marriage relationship each day and each week?"

We all need to ask ourselves the following questions: "What means the most to me?" "As I view the tasks on my priority list, which is the most important thing to do right now?" Individuals have different values, priorities, and pressures. It really boils down to what means the most to us.

Each individual needs to take inventory, on a regular basis, of how he is allocating his time. We should constantly strive to make sure we're spending our time on the things that matter most to us. It is easy to get caught up in the mundane things of the world. It is easy to get caught up in activities that, although may seem important at the time, will most likely have little value to us in the grand scheme of things. Of course, people could state extreme emotions just to manipulate, but if your spouse is feeling neglected, the reality is, he is neglected. It would be easy to say, "Well, that's his problem." However, each spouse should feel like he is the most significant other in his partner's life. When a spouse does not feel that way, strange fantasies and behaviors are entertained, like thinking of other individuals. These thoughts and feelings start to erode the marriage relationship.

If we consider our family the most important thing to us, then our family will receive most of our time. We will not view the family as an intrusion on other important matters. We tend to spend the most time with the things that mean the most to us. This does not mean we'll spend twenty-four hours a day with our family, but our family should be our number-one priority. Most of the time, it is not a matter of choosing between a good and a bad thing, but rather between good things. I have been known to tell members of my family when we make a decision, it is not a 100-percent decision, since the decision is usually made at the exclusion of another good decision.

If a man's wife is preeminent in his life, then he will learn to pace himself and come home with some emotional energy to invest in his wife and family. If he's looking for an excuse not to be a good husband, all he needs to do is come home tired from work and not invest any time or energy into his wife and children. At times each of us does not give the attention to each other we know we should; however, these times should be a rare exception, not the pattern.

My wife and I adopted a motto long ago that we repeat quite often: "It doesn't matter what we do or where we go, as long as we're together." It's logical to believe that the more similarities a couple has regarding their values and priorities, the less friction there will be in their relationship. Ideally, what should a couple's priorities be?

Vaughn J. Featherstone tells the following story:

> The farmer told his wife he was going out to mow the north forty. On his way to the machine shed, he noticed a loose board on the corn crib. So he went to look for a hammer and some nails which he remembered leaving on the back porch. This led him through the garden which he noticed was quite weedy. He decided to weed a row of carrots, telling himself that he ought to weed a row a day. About two-thirds of the way down the carrot row he straightened up to rest his back and, looking over his shoulder, he saw he had left the gate open and some hens had come into the garden and were scratching up his sweet corn. It took about fifteen minutes to get them out and back into the hen yard. It took another half hour to mend the hole through which they were getting out. After that he figured he had just as well gather the eggs. As he began to do so, he noticed that the nests needed more straw; so he left the eggs and went after a bale of straw.
>
> As he was about to pick up the straw, he noticed his pitchfork had a broken handle and remembered that he hadn't fixed it. So he went to the machine shop to hunt for the new handle he had bought. While hunting, he stumbled across the mowing machine and remembered he was going to spend the day mowing. It wasn't much past 10:00 AM; so he decided to return to his original plan. Only he remembered he hadn't greased the mower. He started to hunt for his grease gun. After some searching he remembered that he had left it in the garage. When he found it, it was empty, and he didn't have a refill. So he got in his car and went to town to get some grease.
>
> As he passed Sleepy Corners, he stopped at Sleepy Joe's for a doughnut and a glass of milk. Some of the boys were there, and he learned that the bass were biting down at the reservoir south of town. He got home about lunch time. After lunch, on his way to the machine shed he stumbled over the hoe he had left in the garden. He remembered hoeing up some worms and decided to see if he could find some to set aside for some evening fishing. It didn't take long to get a can of worms. At this point he decided the day was pretty well shot anyway, and he had just as well go fishing right now instead of waiting until evening.[1]

I'm sure we can all relate to this story. The farmer's priority was to mow the north forty. But because of all the distractions and other "good things" he found to do, nothing got accomplished until the end of the day when he went fishing. What happened to his first priority?

Such it is with our marriages and families. We get distracted by many good things, but when it comes right down to it, the essential things don't get done. We have the power within ourselves to make a course correction where needed. Our marriage and family life need to receive more attention.

Q: Family, work, and everything else are piling up. I still love my spouse and we want to spend time together, but we have trouble making time for each other and our relationship. What is a good rule of thumb for making good, quality time for your marital relationship? How can we make it a habit to do more things as a couple?

There are no universal answers to these important questions because ultimately it is up to the couple to make the time. When a couple tells me they don't have time for each other, I sometimes ask them, "Would you spend half an hour together each day and have a meaningful dialogue about family matters if I paid you a thousand dollars a day?" Inevitably, the answer is always a resounding, "Yes!" In essence, if the reward were high enough, they would make the time. There is a difference between *having* the time versus *making* the time to accomplish the essential things in life.

CRISIS VS. VALUES

All of us have a list of values that are extremely important to us. Sometimes we even take them for granted, thinking they will always be there. However, it's usually not until a crisis occurs that we move over to that list of values.

While pursuing my master's degree, I wouldn't have taken five days off if someone offered me five hundred dollars. It may seem odd that a graduate student would decline such an offer. After all, I needed the money; but, doing well on my finals was a much higher priority. Had the person made the same offer after finals, I would've responded differently. Clearly, doing well in graduate school was more important to me than the money.

However, while I was in the middle of finals, I received a phone call that my father had just passed away. Where do you think I was that evening? Although doing well in graduate school was very important, family was an even higher priority to me. I waited until there was a crisis before I moved over to my list of values. As human beings, we all tend to follow this pattern.

A parent asked his children to write Grandma a letter because she would not be alive much longer. The children loved their grandmother but did not have time to write her because they were busy with "important things." Unfortunately, within weeks Grandma died. Now that there was a crisis, this family was able to rearrange their schedule and put their "important things" on hold to attend Grandma's funeral and lend support to their family members. Why do we wait so long to show love, give time, and offer support? Wouldn't it be better if we stepped up our efforts to prioritize our time and not wait until there's a crisis before moving over to that list?

Anything worthwhile takes time and work, but it is worth it. If you want to be good at something, you need to spend whatever time is necessary to get better at it. So it is with marriage. Many believe that once you are in love, you will automatically stay in love; this, of course, is not true. A simple yet accurate analogy is buying a beautiful plant. No one would think of bringing it home and placing it in a hole in the ground with no further attention and still expect it to grow and stay as beautiful as it was when they brought it home. How foolish and unrealistic.

Yet, isn't that similar to how people view marriage? You get married and automatically live happily ever after, without any thought that the marriage might need constant weeding, cultivation, nurturing, and watering.

To help put priorities in perspective, I refer to the following poem.

THE DASH

I read of a man who stood to speak
At the funeral of a friend.
He referred to the dates on her tombstone
From the beginning to the end.

He noted that first came the date of her birth
And spoke the following date with tears,
But he said what mattered most of all
Was the dash between those years.

For that dash represents all the time
That she spent alive on earth.
And now only those who loved her
Know what that little line is worth.

For it matters not how much we own;
The cars, the house, the cash,
What matters is how we live and love
And how we spend our dash.

So think about this long and hard.
Are there things you'd like to change?
For you never know how much time is left,
That can still be rearranged.

If we could just slow down enough
To consider what's true and real
And always try to understand
The way other people feel.

And be less quick to anger,
And show appreciation more
And love the people in our lives
Like we've never loved before.

If we treat each other with respect,
And more often wear a smile
Remembering that this special dash
Might only last a little while.

So, when your eulogy is being read
With your life's actions to rehash
Would you be proud of the things they say
About how you spent your dash?[2]

—Linda Ellis—

Notes

1. Vaughn J. Featherstone, *Commitment* (Salt Lake: Bookcraft Publishing, 1982), 32–33.

2. Quote retrieved from: everyman.org/spirituality/spirituality.html.

The poem "The Dash" appears on pages 172-173. Copyright 1996: Linda Ellis, Linda's Lyrics, www.lindaellis.net

Professional Help: When to Seek It

Q: My husband and I have been married for eight years. We've been through some rough times, and currently we are struggling with many issues in our marriage. He says he doesn't want to be married anymore, but I'm not ready to give up on our relationship, our family, and everything we've built together. How do we know when it is time to seek counseling? What do I do when I want to make this marriage work, and my husband doesn't believe in therapy and wants to throw in the towel? How do I go about choosing a marriage counselor?

DOES MARRIAGE COUNSELING HELP?

An article appearing in *USA Today* in June 1999 mentioned that after two years of marriage counseling, 25 percent of the couples were worse off than before they started therapy. Up to 38 percent of them divorced.[1]

According to William J. Doherty, marriage counseling could even be hazardous to your marriage. He mentions four ways in which marriage counselors can do more harm than good to your marriage:

1. By being incompetent. Not being trained in marriage counseling.
2. By not being neutral. They take sides by using the language of self-interests.
3. By pathologizing (telling you why your marriage is "sick"). They tell the couple that their relationship is not worth the pain it is causing.

4. By being overtly undermining (attempting to break up the marriage). This is accomplished by the therapist saying, "If you're going to stay sane, you should end the marriage."[2]

Not all individuals who practice marriage counseling are licensed. Those who are licensed don't all approach marriage counseling the same. If you don't feel comfortable with the person advising you about your marriage, it may be a good idea to seek out someone else. This is not to say that good counselors should agree with everything you say. In fact, in order to help you as a couple, they shouldn't agree with everything you say, or they will be limited in their ability to help you.

WHEN DOES A MARRIAGE NEED PROFESSIONAL HELP?

A couple should not be too quick to seek out professional help when "normal" disagreements and challenges occur. They cannot give their problems to others to solve. They ultimately have to solve their problems by themselves, with some assistance from others.

A husband and wife working together, each taking responsibility for the difficulties in their relationship and both being committed to do whatever is necessary to improve their relationship, can be successful. It is only when they have exhausted all of their own efforts without success that a third party should be sought. When I see a couple who have put forth considerable effort to solve their problems and are now sitting in front of me embarrassed about seeking help, I reassure them by saying, "If you could have worked out your marital problems on your own, you would have already worked it out and would not be sitting in front of me now."

A couple should generally not share their plight with family or friends. Why? Because for the most part, when marriage problems are shared, the husband and wife will give their "spin" on the problems and orient the listener to *their* perceptions and make it seem as though the spouse is at fault. They will admit that they have some issues too, but essentially they will not admit they are at fault.

Also remember that to live life solely by the advice of professionals is really not to live life at all. Never turn your entire self-determination over to a stranger. This is especially true when the counselor has different values from the couple he is helping.

Finding the Right Professional

When seeking outside help, a couple should ideally find someone who is experienced in marriage counseling and has similar beliefs and values. Find a professional counselor (Licensed Professional Counselor; Licensed Clinical Social Worker; Marriage & Family Therapist; Licensed Psychologist; Psychiatrist) who has his or her head screwed on right. As in any profession, marriage counselors come in a variety of packages. There are some good ones, and then there are those that you would not want to send your worst enemy to. Ask a church leader to help you find the right one. He has probably referred a couple to someone with whom he feels comfortable and about whom he has heard positive things. Talk with family members and with friends, and most likely one or two names of potential counselors will surface. Don't choose someone who will always agree with you. A counselor who agrees with everything that is said will have minimal effect on a couple. It is a false assumption that a person of the same religious denomination as the couple, who has professional initials behind his name, is the most qualified and the most helpful. This is not always the case.

Resisting to Seek Out Help

Some individuals do not want to seek outside help. I've heard people say they wouldn't pay someone money to sit and listen to all their problems. I've heard others say that since they have to solve their own problems anyway, why involve anyone else in their situation? Still, others say it's a sign of weakness to not be able to solve their own problems. Some believe that if you have an emotional illness, all you need to solve the problem is prayer, faith, study, and fasting. Others believe that if a person is living all the commandments, he will have no problems or challenges in his life.

Those responses are not true. We shouldn't have a negative, knee-jerk reaction toward those seeking help. If an individual has a fever, he doesn't necessarily need to see a doctor. However, if his fever still persists after days of trying to overcome it, he may need to make an appointment to see a doctor. If an individual has a toothache for a prolonged period of time, a visit to the dentist would definitely be in order. We usually think nothing of going to someone for medical help, but there is sometimes a negative connotation given toward counseling. The couple's religious leader should be involved in their situation, and both his counsel and his direction should be considered.

Who Benefits Most from Marriage Counseling?

From my experience, the couples that benefit the most from counseling are those who recognize that the marriage is worth saving; those who are committed to each other and are willing to put forth the necessary effort to reconcile their differences. Some factors that can make couple's therapy unsuccessful are waiting too long to seek help, and one of the partners being so set on divorce that he will not even consider going to therapy. If you think your marriage is in trouble, do not wait. Seek professional counseling or attend a marriage course as soon as the warning signs appear.

The following warning signs may indicate that you and your spouse need professional counseling:

- Feeling critical and dissatisfied with each other
- Avoiding each other
- Feeling contempt for one another
- Having conversations that end in arguments, resentment, and defensiveness
- Chronic disagreements about raising your children
- Conflicts ending without resolution
- Bringing up divorce during conflicts
- Dissatisfaction with your intimate relationship
- Withdrawing and avoiding each other
- Recurring fantasies about another person
- Physical or verbal abuse

All of us are counselors to others. Each individual has challenges and trials. Each of us has been asked for our advice or opinion. Keep in mind some of the following ideas when you are put in such a situation:

1. Be more of a facilitator than a source. Try and help the other person come up with a solution to his problems, and remember that teaching him how to fish will be more beneficial to him than providing him a fish for one day.
2. Be on guard. Don't let others dump their problems on you and make you feel responsible for them.
3. Learn how to step out of your frame of reference without giving it up in order to help someone who is presenting a very sensitive issue.

4. We are responsible to *help* other people rather than being responsible *for* other people.

Notes

1. K. S. Petersen, "Couples therapists offer many paths to happily ever after. Joint sessions can steer marriage back from brink," *USA Today,* 29 Jun. 1999.

2. William J. Doherty, *Take Back Your Marriage: Sticking Together in a World that Pulls Us Apart,* (New York: Guilford Press, 2003), 95–100.

Roles

Q: A fair number of people are against the typical roles of women and men in today's society. How can roles in a marriage and family be used to a family's advantage?

Q: I want to help my wife more with the responsibilities around the house, but sometimes she doesn't allow me to help. I'll ask her what I can do, but it's almost like she's guarding the tasks that need to be done so that they will be done the way she likes. This "task guarding" is causing other problems for us. How can I help my wife understand how important it is to me to share responsibilities?

Many evolving theories and practices are being promoted as "the right roles" for men and women to adopt. Some even say, "Whatever works, works!" How is one to know which roles, practices, and beliefs are correct?

Married couples have the opportunity to help one another as equal partners within individual roles. Each family has individual circumstances that require different fulfillment of these roles.

When a couple begins their marriage, each has an anticipatory perception as to what role they will occupy in the relationship. The more this expectation is adhered to, the less friction there will be in the relationship. But when a spouse wants their partner to perform in a role that he is not comfortable with or didn't anticipate, more marital friction results. I have also noticed that the better the couple can communicate concerning these different role perceptions and expectations, the more satisfying their marriage will be. The sharing of roles is helpful to attain a higher level of marital satisfaction.

I once worked with a couple where the husband would not help with tasks in the kitchen. His father didn't do it, his brothers didn't do it in their marriages, and he was not going to be the first to do so. When his wife asked for help, he would reply, "I will not." No matter what she did or how she begged, he would not help. His behavior and preconceived ideas of what his role was had caused great marital strife. There were some definite adjustments that needed to be made within this relationship for it to survive.

However, in our daily life tasks, we have the opportunity to build our relationships with one another. Family and housework never go away. Involving the entire family in housework and turning tasks into fun competitions or games will help improve family relationships, convey the message of caring and cooperation, and keep the home running smoothly. Involving the whole family in the several facets of work may not be the most efficient way to complete a task, but relationships are built and maintained through helping family relationships become stronger and more united.

In order to prove that women can do everything a man can do, supporters of the feminist movement forgot to elevate the divine role of women as nurturers and caretakers of the home. If the roles of nurturing, motherhood, and caring for the home and family had been more emphasized and seen as the vital roles they are, men and women would be better able to appreciate masculine and feminine roles and contributions to society. By insisting that women get to do the exact same activities as men, the feminist movement actually elevated the masculine roles in society and devalued the traditional, time-honored, God-given roles of women.

Self-Awareness

Q: I work with some individuals who have, in my opinion, some negative personal characteristics that I don't want to make part of my life. They appear to either not care, or they aren't aware of how they come across to others. Lack of self-awareness or ambivalence to others' perceptions would have to be destructive to their marriages and families. I want to improve my self-awareness so I don't get caught in their same traps. I'd also like to correct some of my thinking and attitudes.

DEVELOPING SELF-AWARENESS

Even though most people believe they have self-awareness, I believe most don't. I once pointed out to a graduate student I was working with a mannerism I detected in his counseling. He replied, "That can't be the case; that has never been pointed out to me before and I am not aware of it." I then proceeded to rewind the video of his session, and sure enough, the mannerism was shown again on the monitor. He was stunned. This was the first time this behavior had been brought to his attention. He had been recorded numerous times, and nothing had been said to him.

To begin developing self-awareness, ask yourself the following questions:

1. What are my strengths?
2. What are my weaknesses?
3. Am I a good listener?
4. Do I interrupt people when they're talking to me?
5. Do I like to lecture others with my knowledge?

6. Do I get feedback from others about my personal qualities and characteristics, but deny their existence?
7. Do I have to be right all the time?
8. Do people come to me for advice, or do they avoid me?
9. Do I always have to be in the limelight?
10. Am I comfortable giving credit to others?

These and other questions will provide an opportunities for an individual to honestly look in the mirror and evaluate himself. Self-awareness can lead to self-correction. If someone else tries to change you, you may become resentful and argumentative. In some cases, pride is a major factor. Their has to be a balance between confidence and pride; humbleness and shyness. You do not want to appear *so* confident that others perceive you as conceited. If you like what you see when you look in the mirror, and feedback from significant others reinforces our positive qualities, continue to develop those over the years. If you do not like what you see when you look in the mirror, and that view coincides with comments significant others make, then make some changes. If you are not sure how you come across to others, seek out someone that you trust and ask him for feedback. This is risky but is a very important step in developing self-awareness.

It's important that a husband is aware of how he comes across to his wife. The best way to discover this is to ask her, but he must not be defensive when she answers. It may also be helpful for him to get feedback from other significant individuals in his life and be willing to listen to their feedback.

Selfishness

Q: My husband is a fun-loving guy who likes to be the life of the party. In fact, if he hasn't been the center of attention at a party or get-together, he later complains that it was boring. When we talk, it has to be about him and his concerns, or we do not talk at all. His willingness to talk about himself, and his ability to make people laugh were some of the qualities that attracted me to him in the first place; now they just push me away. I feel like I'm a piece of furniture, rather than the most important person in his life. What can I do to help him see how selfish he's being?

Selfishness is thinking of yourself before anyone else. It is being self-centered. It is taking care of your wants and desires first, and if there is any time left and something in it for you, you will then focus on someone else. Putting yourself first is destructive to a marriage.

When a couple marries, there are many advantages and there are some disadvantages. In other words, you win some things and you lose some things. One of the disadvantages or losses of getting married is that an individual cannot think entirely of himself. There is a significant other in his life and her comfort needs to come before his own. Selflessness, the ability to do things for your spouse without the expectation of getting anything in return is at the hallmark of a successful marriage.

When married, to think of yourself first is something that can be destructive to the marriage. I'm reminded of a man who, shortly after his wedding, wanted to continue his athletic involvement in numerous city and church sports teams. He was involved as either a coach or a player, which consumed a considerable amount of his time. These activities consumed three or four nights a week. He and his buddies would play various kinds of videos games or participate in other types of activities into the early morning hours. As a result of his involvement with these various activities, his wife felt that she was not a priority to him. He could not understand her feelings. He always told her that he loved her, and even invited her to some of his athletic activities.

It can easily be seen by some that this husband was not willing to think of or put his wife before his activities. He was being very selfish with this time by spending his spare time on himself rather than thinking of his wife. In one of my interviews with him, he told me he didn't understand why his wife was so upset with him.

Thinking of others first rather than yourself, especially in marriage, is a sign of emotional maturity and a positive self-concept. In a marriage relationship, thinking in terms of "we" and "us" is healthier than being selfish and just think about "me." Thinking of your spouse before yourself and meeting his needs before your needs is a sign of maturity and of a healthy relationship. It is a basic, core quality that is needed for a successful marriage.

Service

Q: I often get tired of telling my husband every little thing that I need him to help me do. I would like him to discover that he needs to look for things that need to be done and do them, rather than leaving them for me all the time. How can I help him see that service is a big part of a successful marriage? How can I help him understand that I would like him to be more helpful on his own accord?

Service is the manifestation of a selfless person, and it takes a lot of maturity. However, it's an essential characteristic for both partners to possess in order to make the marriage better.

As fundamental as it sounds, selflessness and service is the golden rule in action. If the partners in a relationship will treat each other how they would like to be treated, they will be happy.

When a couple marries, they're saying to each other, "I will love you forever." However, the meaning of these words is seriously impaired if serving each other is not included in their actions. Service in marriage suggests a commitment to the welfare of your spouse as well as a willing acceptance of the role of a servant.

If a spouse is more concerned about the comfort, well-being, and meeting the needs of his partner rather than his own, the marriage is doing very well.

When we serve others, we are doing something for them instead of for ourselves. When we are sacrificing for others, we are serving them by helping to meet their needs and their wants. In some cases, we're doing for them that which they cannot do for themselves. We often sacrifice (or give of) our time, talents, possessions, and means to assist someone else. When we serve others, we experience a warm, satisfying feeling that conveys to us that we have done the right thing.

When you are serving your spouse, there is no room for selfishness.

Sensitivity

Q: Recently my husband and I have been arguing a great deal. He is not as sensitive to my needs as he was when we were dating. He used to anticipate my needs and make sure I was able to express all my concerns. Now I'm upset because my feelings and needs don't come first anymore, and I feel resentful toward him. What can I do to appropriately express my frustration toward him?

Q: I have been struggling to get along with my husband, Ralph. It all started awhile ago when my health began to decline and I became unable to do a lot of things I was once able to do. I have less energy than I used to, and as a result, I take longer to do my work. Ralph was really understanding for a little while, but now says I should be able to take care of things on my own. I have tried working harder, but my doctor says that if I push too hard, my problems could worsen. How can I help Ralph understand that I need him to care for me and be more sensitive to the difficulties I am experiencing?

There are two main components to this question:

1) What is the physical problem the wife is experiencing? She only refers to it as "my health" and does not mention anything specific. The husband should hear directly from the doctor what the source of the problem is, what her diagnosis is, and what the prognosis is. It would also be important for the doctor to tell the husband directly how he could best help his wife. Obtaining this information should help the husband realize that his wife's problem is real, not imaginary. Of course, the husband

needs to rearrange his priorities and listen when his wife says he is not sensitive to her and is not concerned about her or her difficulties. He also needs to be more sensitive, understanding, compassionate, and more willing to listen to his wife's comments. It would be very easy for the husband to say "this is her problem, not mine." However, if your spouse has a problem, you have a problem too. Here, the wife is personalizing her husband's lack of attention to her. As a result, she feels like he doesn't love her. Even if he does not agree with how his wife is conducting herself, his responsibility is to be compassionate and more attentive to her circumstances and needs.

2) The health problem is creating limitations on the amount of energy the wife has. When she works harder, she pays the price of fatigue. The wife will have to develop new boundaries for the amount of work she is able to do and stick with it, whether the husband approves or not.

How can one start thinking of his spouse more than himself? I think it happens in small steps, on a day-to-day basis. Maybe he realizes she's tired, so he puts the kids to bed, or he pitches in somewhere else without being asked. This is when things begin to click. A wife feels closest to her husband when he's more sensitive to her needs than he is to his own. The husband may say to himself, "I'm tired, but I know she's really tired too. I'll take the kids to the park, and she can have an hour to herself tonight." For him to do that without being asked shows his wife that he loves her, even though he's tired and just wants to sit down and relax. It's doing the little things that make the relationship stronger.

Quite frequently in my practice, I hear one spouse say to the other, "It's your problem, not mine." Frankly, this is a very selfish attitude. The process begins by empathizing with your spouse and the pain he is experiencing, even though you're not personally experiencing the pain yourself. A parent would not say to his child who has just fallen and hurt his knee, "Why are you crying? I'm not in pain, so stop your crying right now." Just ask yourself, "How would I want to be treated if I felt the way my spouse does?" If this type of attitude is not developed, resentment will begin to fester, and callousness will result in the relationship.

Do not keep a scorecard and meticulously keep track of the things you do for your spouse, or constantly remind him what deeds have been done. These deeds should be done in a selfless manner, without playing the martyr.

NEED FOR EMPATHY AND ATTENTIVENESS

Q: My husband, Jeremy, and I have three small children, all under the age of six. I love my husband and my children, but I sometimes feel so alone. Jeremy works long hours and goes to school at night. I have been staying home with our children, but sometimes I need more support. I realize I've become resentful, unfeeling, and insensitive in so many aspects of my marriage. I realize Jeremy is busy, but how can I learn to show empathy and become more thoughtful of his pressures, yet also help him understand that I need more of his support in raising our family?

Achieving success in the home is a great challenge and goal. Unless a husband and wife learn to work together as one, marriage can be a grind. There are too many unhappy marriages in the world today. There are too many marriages that do not stay the course, that end prematurely in divorce. There are too many children who are silently suffering from a lack of nurturing and care because their parents' union is unhappy or dissolved.

Lack of empathy in a relationship enables thoughtlessness and a lack of sensitivity. When you can't identify with what your spouse is feeling, you tend to ignore the negative effects you have on your spouse. The inflictor of the pain usually does not feel the pain.

I try to encourage spouses to avoid pushing each other's buttons. I have a difficult time creating empathy or caring within each spouse when they both complain about how hurtful, thoughtless, and lacking in feeling the other is, with little or no insight into his or her own actions.

Empathy must begin by relinquishing the feeling of entitlement and justification to blame the other, and taking a look at one's own behavior. It is often said that the only person we can change is ourselves, and this is the case with empathy. First, we must recognize what we can do about our own behavior so we can improve the situation, and then we can move forward and focus on showing concern for others. Empathy is the ability to accurately understand the thoughts, feelings, attitudes, orientation, and experience of another person. It is a feature of both love and righteous power.

Just before a father walks in the door, if he will say to himself, "I am now a father and husband, *then* a student and employee," his focus will change from himself to his wife and children and their needs. This has to be a conscious decision every day. If he does this, he will see great changes and improvement in his marriage.

Single Life

Q: I am thirty-six years old and have always been shy. I believe I have good interpersonal skills and I'm easy to talk to, but when I'm on a date, I seem to freeze up and I rarely act myself. I can't seem to find someone I like and can act normal around. I have been in a few relationships before, but they didn't seem right for one reason or another. I would like to get married, but I almost don't know how to go about it. I participate in all of the singles activities, but Mr. Right hasn't shown up yet. What advice do you have for single persons looking to get married?

Being single is only one aspect of your entire self. Often, however, when describing a person who is single, he is thought of only in relation to his marital status. Why don't we refer to them as to who they are as a person, or to his other characteristics?

All of us have been single during our lifetime. Being single affords each of us the opportunity to become self-reliant and to discover who we are and what we do and don't like, how we deal with things, what we want out of life, what our expectations are, what our potential and limitations are, what empowers us, and what discourages and disappoints us. Being alone shouldn't *only* prepare us for marriage. The purpose of entering into a relationship is to share oneself with another person, not to get from them what we are lacking in ourselves.

While we are single, we can develop qualities such as kindness, maturity, patience, and charity, instead of waiting until we are married. I refer to some words from the newspaper column *Dear Abby*:

The key to being popular with both sexes is: Be kind. Be honest. Be tactful. If you can't be beautiful (or handsome), be well-groomed, tastefully attired, conscious of your posture, and keep a smile on your face.

Be clean in body and mind. If you're not a "brain," try harder. If you're not a great athlete, be a good sport. Try to be a standout in something. If you can't dance or sing, learn to play an instrument. Think for yourself, but respect the rules. Be generous with kind words and affectionate gestures, but save the heavy artillery. . . . You'll be glad you did.[1]

In other words, a person's future is in his own hands. Instead of just focusing on marital status as the barometer for success in life, look for opportunities to constantly improve. This can be accomplished through education, career development, and personal enrichment activities. Some people will never marry in this life, yet they are well-rounded, well-adjusted, fascinating people. There is nothing wrong with you if you are single; however, there is something wrong if you are obsessed with just getting married and ignore many other aspects of your life.

Notes

1.   "Dear Abby," reprinted in *Chicago Tribune*, 17 Mar. 1991, 6.

Special Occasions

Q: When I was growing up, my father didn't acknowledge special days such as birthdays, anniversaries, or Valentine's Day. It was up to my mother to take the lead in the celebrations. My wife is very good at remembering my birthday, our children's birthdays, and other important days throughout the year. She wants to celebrate special events the same way her family did when she was growing up. Personally, I think some of these ways are silly, and I would like to celebrate them differently. I have now been married for seven years, and I've forgotten to plan or do anything for my wife's birthday or Valentine's Day for the past four years. I get so involved with my work and other projects that I forget, and I'm not always available to celebrate family members' birthdays or other special events. It takes a lot of time to plan meaningful activities on the special days, and it is time I do not have. I know that forgetting these special occasions really hurts my wife. I try to tell her that I have plenty other days throughout the year to show her that I love her, but that doesn't seem to remove the disappointment. What ideas do you have to help forgetful husbands like me to remember special days and occasions?

There are three main aspects to this question that need to be addressed.

1. Do newly married couples need to carry on the traditions of their upbringing?
2. Can new traditions be established?
3. Can you make time to celebrate special events?

First, newly married couples come from families where holidays and special days are remembered and celebrated differently. After marriage, the celebration needs to continue, even though it might be in a way one of the partners is not accustomed to. Holidays and special occasions are great times to develop family traditions and rituals. Always keep in mind that how you celebrate the special events is not as important as just celebrating them.

Second, there is nothing wrong with wanting to remember and incorporate some of the things your family did while you were growing up. At the same time, there's value in creating new traditions and rituals. It's a matter of thinking outside the box. Is it possible that some of the old traditions could remain, while allowing room for new ones? Yes.

For example, when I was growing up, Christmas morning was over and done with by 7:30 AM. The children woke up first, then our parents, and we would all rush into the living room and tear open the packages. For the first few years of my married life, Christmas morning occurred the same way. But in discussing the matter with my wife, we soon came to realize that a lot of effort went into the preparation of Christmas morning, and we needed to enjoy it more than we had been. Over the years, with the children's input and further discussion between my wife and me, Christmas morning has evolved into our own unique pattern. We take our time. We have our traditional Christmas breakfast, we discuss the meaning of Christmas, and then we open presents one at a time. After a present is open, the receiver gives a hug to the giver of the present. We are in no hurry, and sometimes we're not through opening presents until mid-afternoon. Some years this process needs to be altered, but we want to enjoy the day and be relaxed. After all, a lot of time and energy has gone into making this day special. Why not enjoy it?

Third, in referring back to the question stated at the beginning of the chapter, the husband needs to realize that even though the celebration of significant days may not be important to him, he needs to understand how important it is to his wife.

It would be easy for the husband to say that his wife is overreacting and that the children are making a big deal about him not remembering special days or events. However, if a pattern of forgetfulness is established, most wives and children will feel hurt and unappreciated.

In today's world it is much easier to be organized and remember significant events. Any type of scheduler (calendar, electronic calendar, cell phone, or computer) can assist a forgetful mind with upcoming special events. Just think for a moment: If the husband's boss asked for a particular project to be turned in by a certain date, the boss would become very upset if the worker came to him and stated, "I'm sorry, but I just forgot." Most likely, the worker would take whatever steps necessary to remember the due date. With that same tenacity, the husband needs to realize that special days become opportunities to express appreciation to the significant people in his life. These days are just as important as remembering deadlines given to him at work.

The husband should take whatever steps are necessary to plan ahead and demonstrate his love and appreciation to the significant people in his life. Special days and events help connect family members to each other. I once heard a husband say that he felt that stating his love for his wife on special occasions was contrived. He felt he could show his love to his wife more throughout the year, rather than just on one day. In reality, he did not show his love at all. If love is only expressed on special occasions, the marriage has problems. On the other hand, if the love is not stated on special days, the marriage is in trouble. These special days provide opportunities for a husband and wife to remind each other of their love and respect. It's worth the investment to remind our loved ones of our love for them, and to show our children how important it is to express our love for each other. In a world that is trying to pull the family apart, acknowledging special individuals on special days becomes the glue that holds a family together. It also provides memories for the children to build upon as they grow older and establish traditions and rituals in their own families. It *can* be done. It *must* be done.

Spiritual Perspective

Q: Physical and emotional aspects are often addressed regarding marriage. How important is the spiritual perspective?

Most married couples would likely say they didn't meet by accident, but by divine intervention. Someone once said that with God, there are no surprises. What we as mortal beings label as coincidence might have been God's plan for us all along. This is not to say that human beings do not have moral agency and as such can blindly make wrong decisions. However, a religious individual who has a prayer in his heart and tries to do the will of God will be aided in making decisions.

Marriage is ordained of God and is very important to Him. Therefore, it seems logical that He would guide an individual to a marriage partner, and assist him in carrying out his life's plan. This is not to say that there is a "one and only," but rather that divine intervention and assistance play very important roles at the beginning of this important association. This explains why most individuals contemplating a marriage partner will seek special guidance and spiritual confirmation.

No matter what denomination a person adheres to, a spiritual influence can help a couple in their relationship.

DEVELOPING A SPIRITUAL PERSPECTIVE

It is imperative that couples have a spiritual perspective of their relationship and their potential as a couple. The world does not provide that perspective. Achieving marital harmony takes tremendous patience and persistence and a clear idea of what our priorities are in this life and in the life after.

A dissertation entitled *The Relationship of Spirituality and Marital Satisfaction Among Roman Catholic Couples* provides insight into the importance of having a spiritual perspective in a marital relationship. The dissertation reveals four significant predictors of marital satisfaction:

1. Discussing God's role in the marriage with one's spouse.
2. Praying daily with one's spouse.
3. Observing fasts/holy days together.
4. Believing that marriage helps one's spiritual growth and that God is experienced in marriage.[1]

A spiritual perspective is basically having a "big picture" of what life is all about. For each couple, that picture is different. It's looking beyond today and looking to next week, next month, next year, or five to ten years from now. It is asking ourselves, "What will the impact of my decision and behavior today have on my life and my family's life in the future, even after I die?"

Having a spiritual perspective can assist the couple when challenges face them. Whether there are small or large disagreements, or stress in the family relationship, maintaining a spiritual perspective will aid each spouse in incorporating the Christlike qualities necessary to placing an earthly occurrence into a spiritual perspective. By keeping this perspective, life's occurrences can be kept in perspective and prioritized.

Notes

1. Stanislaw J. Strycharz, "Dissertation Abstracts International: Section B" *The Sciences and Engineering*, Vol. 64, 2004, 8B.

Trust

Q: My husband has violated my trust several times, but I would like to rebuild the trust we once had. How can we do this?

Trust is crucial to the success of any marital relationship. I remember counseling a couple in which the husband had been involved in behaviors that were not conducive to building trust. He told me he didn't believe his wife was aware of his behaviors, nor did his actions have a negative impact on the marriage. Later, when I talked to the wife in private, she indicated that she was aware of her husband's behavior and that his conduct *was* having a negative impact on the marriage, especially on her feelings toward him. The only reason she was not confronting him with her perceptions was that she was hoping he would come to his senses and realize the price he was paying for his behavior.

His behavior did not include pornography, infidelity, or flirtations. Rather, it had to do with secretly spending money and not giving an account of it. It had to do with telling his wife he was going to be at one location but then spending his time at another location. It had to do with telling his wife he had to work overtime, when in reality he got off work early to hang out with some of his buddies. It had to do with constantly catching him in white lies. Basically, the wife had learned over the years to always question what he said. She didn't know when to believe him.

The question needs to be asked, "Why is the husband being untruthful?" A person who is untruthful is pretending to be someone he's not. He believes that if the truth were discovered, no one would like him. Some type of justification is always used. He needs to take a long, hard look in the mirror and realize that what he's doing is destructive to a healthy marital relationship. When he realizes this, and when the barriers are lowered, the couple can make progress to trust each other again.

Trust is one of the major foundation stones of a successful marriage. Without it, the relationship can erode. Unless the crack of mistrust is repaired, all the effort and energy focused on the relationship will be defused and siphoned out.

The following are suggestions of how trust can be increased:

- Regularly convey your sincere feelings of appreciation to your spouse.
- When you say you'll do something, do it.
- When you say you are going somewhere, go there and come right back.
- Anticipate your spouse's needs, and then do your best to meet them.
- Constantly give to the marital relationship.
- Keep the communication lines open.
- If your spouse says that she doesn't trust you, change immediately.
- If anything you do is offensive to your spouse, stop it.
- Make sure your spouse is your best friend and you want to spend time together.
- Don't let relationships outside the marital relationship get out of hand.
- Don't let flirtations or infatuations be confused with real, committed love.
- Do not get over-emotionally involved with individuals who are going through stressful times and dumping their problems on you.

Besides an explicit change of behavior by the offending party, the other spouse needs to be forgiving. When two partners in a marital relationship establish trust, they develop a secure attachment and positive marital attitudes between each other. Then trust can begin to develop.

About the Author

Kenneth W. Matheson, a Professor in the School of Social Work at Brigham Young University, earned master's and doctorate degrees in social work from the University of Utah. He is a licensed marriage and family therapist and clinical social worker, and has been involved in clinical practice for over forty years. Ken has lectured and presented numerous marriage seminars across the country, and has published in various books and magazines dealing with marriage and family. He has served on advisory boards for various agencies and been a member of a board of education for twelve years. He and his wife, Marlene, are the parents of six children and grandparents of five.